INTERPRETING AND ANALYZING

FINANCIAL STATEMENTS

THIRD EDITION

KAREN P. SCHOENEBECK

Upper Saddle River, New Jersey 07458

Library of Congress Cataloging-in-Publication information is available.

Acquisitions Editor: Bill Larkin
Editor-in-Chief: P. J. Boardman
Editorial Assistant: Jane Avery
Marketing Manager: Beth Toland
Marketing Assistant: Patrick Danzuso
Managing Editor: John Roberts
Production Assistant: Joe DeProspero
Manufacturing Buyer: Michelle Klein
Cover Design: C2K, Inc.
Cover Photo: Janis Christie / Getty Images, Inc. — Photodisc
Printer/Binder: R. R. Donnelly–Willard

Pearson Education LTD.
Pearson Education Singapore, Pte. Ltd
Pearson Education, Canada, Ltd
Pearson Education–Japan

Pearson Education Australia PTY, Limited
Pearson Education North Asia Ltd
Pearson Educación de Mexico, S.A. de C.V.
Pearson Education Malaysia, Pte. Ltd

10 9 8 7 6 5 4 3 2
ISBN 0-13-008216-3

TABLE OF CONTENTS

CHAPTER 3: ANALYZING THE INCOME STATEMENT

CHAPTER 5: FURTHER RATIO ANALYSIS

CHAPTER 6: INTERPRETING AND UNDERSTANDING SPECIFIC ACCOUNTS

CHAPTER 7: COMPREHENSIVE REVIEW

CHAPTER 8: EXCEL SHPREADSHEET APPLICATIONS

CHAPTER 10: CORPORATE ANALYSIS

PREFACE

While this book can be used to supplement any financial accounting text, the activities have been designed to accompany *Financial Accounting*, 5th edition, by Walter T. Harrison, Jr., and Charles T. Horngren (Prentice Hall, 2004).

WHY THESE ACTIVITIES WERE DEVELOPED

When I first started assigning a comprehensive financial statement analysis as a capstone project, it became evident many students didn't know where to begin. They were overwhelmed by all of the numbers and felt frustrated. As a result, this series of preliminary activities was developed to prepare students for the capstone project. Each activity concentrates on only one aspect of financial statement analysis. After completing the preliminary activities, students feel confident in their strategies and ability to successfully complete a comprehensive financial statement analysis.

USING DATA FROM WELL-KNOWN CORPORATIONS

These activities use financial data from companies familiar to students. The actual numbers make the class relevant and more interesting to students. Because students are already familiar with the companies, they more easily grasp the material and remember the concepts.

FOCUS IS ON INTERPRETING AND ANALYZING

Most amounts are provided and calculations are kept to a minimum so students can focus their time and attention on interpretation and analysis. Fifteen minutes on average is required for completion of each activity.

RATIO ANALYSIS

Activities point out the significant role ratios have in analyzing financial statements. Students acquire a "feel" for the expected range and magnitude of the ratios and identify whether a high or low ratio is usually preferred. Commonly used ratios are studied.

TREND PERCENTAGES AND COMMON-SIZE STATEMENT ANALYSIS

Trend percentages are used to evaluate both the income statement and the balance sheet. Emphasis is placed on comparing the rate of increase or decrease of various account classifications within each financial statement. Common-size statements are used to compare companies of different size.

EXCEL SPREADSHEETS

Financial statements are prepared and analyzed using Excel spreadsheets. To reinforce understanding, students are required to prepare formulas to create common-size statements, trend percentages, and ratios. A comparative analysis of two companies is used to demonstrate the effectiveness of Excel formulas. An Excel graph is created in one activity and then pulled into a PowerPoint presentation. Excel techniques introduced provide valuable tools for successful completion of the comprehensive analysis project and presentation in Chapter 10.

INTERNET RESEARCH

Internet activities are used to introduce a comprehensive set of websites offering financial information while also requiring financial statement analysis. These Internet websites provide valuable sources of information for successful completion of the comprehensive analysis project in Chapter 10.

OTHER RESEARCH

Other research activities require reading *The Wall Street Journal*, calling a local bank, or utilizing library resources that are available. The final chapter contains a corporate analysis that requires in-depth research of a company. These research activities expose students to a variety of resources available to help with gathering financial information.

FOUR-YEAR COMPARISON

Financial statements are introduced using four years of comparative information. Each line item is studied and the student develops an overall strategy to analyze the financial statement. Questions lead to increased understanding and highlight important trends.

ETHICAL ISSUES

Ethical issues are incorporated into a number of the activities.

RANGE AND MAGNITUDE OF AMOUNTS

Companies are carefully selected so students get a "feel" for the range and magnitude of expected amounts and ratios in the corporate world.

REVIEW

Review exercises titled "Test Your Understanding" are located at the end of most chapters. In addition, Chapter 6 provides a thorough review of each balance sheet account and Chapter 7 provides a comprehensive review of all the financial statements.

CLASS FORMAT

These activities can be utilized as individual homework assignments, small-group discussions in class, a review, or a combination of all three. Whichever approach is used, these assignments result in thorough understanding and lively classroom discussion.

CORPORATE RESEARCH AND ANALYSIS

The final project requires students to research, analyze, and prepare a comprehensive written report and presentation on the public corporation of their choice. To complete the project, students must obtain a copy of the corporate financial statements and utilize a variety of resources. Because the company is the student's choice, interest is high and a quality product results. This project has several parts. The parts may be assigned throughout the semester, or as a capstone project at the end of the semester.

TO THE INSTRUCTOR...

This book contains a series of activities designed to help students acquire the necessary skills to interpret, analyze, and research financial statement information. A user-oriented approach is maintained throughout the book, utilizing financial information from companies familiar to students. For successful completion of the problem materials, both a conceptual understanding and mathematical computations are required. Activities employ written exercises, Internet activities, and other research opportunities to strengthen understanding. Ethical issues are raised. With over 100 activities to choose from, instructors can select activities appropriate to their needs.

Chapter 1 is designed to accompany the first few weeks of a semester course. Basic accounting concepts are reinforced. An early introduction of ratios, trend analysis, and common-size statements enhance understanding of the relationship between amounts on the balance sheet and the income statement throughout the course. The analysis activities require no previous introduction.

Chapters 2, 3, and 4 are designed as a step-by-step guide for analyzing each of the three major financial statements. Questions lead to increased understanding and highlight important trends. These activities can be assigned anytime after the first few weeks of a semester course. They can be used concurrently with the financial statement coverage in the text, after the statement coverage as a review to reinforce understanding, or simply as a stand-alone assignment at any point throughout the semester. The activities in these chapters start basic and progress to more complex.

Chapter 5 introduces industry norms for the ratios and reviews thirteen commonly used ratios. Ratios from well-known corporations provide the foundation for activity questions.

Chapter 6 should be used throughout the semester as the topics arise. Specific balance sheet account information is presented followed by a series of questions that test for understanding. A thorough understanding of the material is required for successful completion. The later activities examine the stock and bond markets, which enhance the coverage of liabilities and stockholders' equity.

Chapter 7 provides a comprehensive review of all three major financial statements. The activities review understanding of transaction analysis, finding specific account information, interpreting financial information, and analyzing all three major financial statements.

Chapter 8 introduces the use of Excel spreadsheets for analysis. Excel is used to prepare condensed financial statements, common-size statements, trend percentages, ratios, and graphs. These activities prepare the student for the comprehensive analysis project and presentation in Chapter 10.

Chapter 9 introduces Internet research and those websites that are most helpful in locating financial information and then using the information to analyze a specific company. These activities prepare the student for the research required to complete the comprehensive analysis project in Chapter 10.

Chapter 10 is a Corporate Analysis project with six parts. It can be assigned as a capstone project at the end of the semester or as a series of assignments spread throughout the semester. This final project requires students to research, analyze, and prepare a comprehensive, written report or presentation on the public corporation of their choice. This project provides an opportunity to apply and reinforce learning from all previous activities and from the accounting course.

Have fun with these assignments. Bring real-world numbers into the classroom in an organized series of assignments. My students enjoy these assignments and the learning that results. I hope you do too. Please feel free to contact me with comments and questions regarding these activities. My e-mail address is kschoene@sckans.edu.

Karen Schoenebeck, author

TO THE STUDENT...

WARNING!!!
MANY OF THE QUESTIONS CONTAINED IN THIS BOOK REQUIRE THOUGHT!

You are about to embark on a journey into the world of business. Some of you read *The Wall Street Journal* on a regular basis, while others have not yet been introduced to assets and liabilities. This series of activities is designed to introduce you to the financial information for a variety of familiar companies and financial statement analysis. After completing these activities you should feel confident in your ability to research and understand any set of corporate financial statements. Below is a summary of each chapter followed by a question answered in the chapter material.

Chapter 1 introduces the range and magnitude of amounts reported on financial statements of well-known companies. Ratios, trend percentages, and common-size statements are introduced. *For major corporations, are sales usually reported in the range of millions, billions, or trillions?*

Chapters 2, 3, and 4 introduce strategies for analyzing the financial statements and then apply those strategies. Trend percentages and common-size statements are prepared and followed by questions that lead to interpretation and understanding.
Chapter 2: *Does an increase in retained earnings indicate the company issued more stock, purchased more assets, or reported net income?*
Chapter 3: *If sales increase by 10%, would you also expect expenses to increase?*
Chapter 4: *The primary source of cash for an established company with a strong cash position should be operating, investing, or financing activities?*

Chapter 5 reinforces the information provided by various financial ratios and introduces industry norms. An understanding of ratios is developed and whether an increasing or decreasing trend is usually preferred. *Industry average information is reported using which four-digit code?*

Chapter 6 reinforces understanding amounts reported on the financial statements. It also examines the stock and bond market and benchmarks current interest rates and the Dow Jones Industrial Average. Research activities require use of *The Wall Street Journal. For property, plant, and equipment (PPE), is acquisition cost or book value added to calculate total assets?*

Chapter 7 provides a comprehensive review of all three major financial statements. The activities review understanding of transaction analysis, finding specific account information, interpreting financial information, and analyzing all three major financial statements. *When using LIFO, the most recent (current) inventory costs are reported on which financial statement?*

Chapter 8 introduces the use of Excel spreadsheets for analysis. Excel is used to prepare condensed financial statements, common-size statements, trend percentages, ratios, and graphs. These activities prepare the student for the Corporate Analysis project in Chapter 10. *Did revenues or net income increase at a greater rate for the Fuji Photo Film Co., Ltd., since 3/31/99?*

Chapter 9 introduces Internet research and those websites that are most helpful in locating financial information and then using the information to analyze a specific company. These activities prepare the student for the research required to complete the Corporate Analysis in Chapter 10. *Does Coca-Cola report more domestic or international sales?*

Chapter 10 is a comprehensive project that requires researching and analyzing a publicly traded corporation of your choice.

ABOUT THE AUTHOR

KAREN SCHOENEBECK, C.P.A., received her M.B.A. from the University of Minnesota.

EMPLOYMENT HISTORY includes:
- Public accounting experience with Baird, Kurtz, and Dobson in Kansas and Shinners, Hucovski, and Company, S.C. in Wisconsin.
- More than fifteen years of teaching experience at Wichita State University, St. Norbert College in Wisconsin, and currently for Southwestern College of Kansas.
- Administrative experience as M.B.A. Program Director.

PUBLISHED AUTHOR of accounting books and supplementary materials published by Prentice Hall including:
- Karen Schoenebeck, *Test Item File*, to accompany *Cost Accounting: A Managerial Emphasis*, eleventh edition, by Horngren, Datar, and Foster published by Prentice Hall, 2003. (833 pages)
- Karen Schoenebeck and Linda Christensen, *Test Item File*, to accompany *Management Accounting*, third edition, by Atkinson, Banker, Kaplan, and Young published by Prentice Hall, 2002. (450 pages)

LEADERSHIP TRAINING PRACTITIONER presenting at more than 10 national conferences on topics that include *Resolving Ethical Issues, Negotiating Conflict Situations, Essential Skills for Managing Change, Management Styles, Collaborative Skills: Building Effective Teams, Facilitation Skills, Presentation Skills, and Mentoring Relationships.*

SERVICE TO PROFESSIONAL ORGANIZATIONS includes nine years of service on national board of directors of various accounting organizations and for the 1999-2000 term as National President of the Educational Foundation for Women in Accounting.

TRAVEL AND THE ARTS Karen is a docent at the Wichita Art Museum and has experienced different cultures through independent travel to over twenty-five countries in Europe, Asia, and North America. Recently, she spent six weeks traveling independently throughout Asia.

ACKNOWLEDGMENTS

I WOULD LIKE TO THANK...

The Prentice Hall staff including Deborah Hoffman who discovered my materials, encouraged me to submit them for publishing, and continues to support my work; Jane Avery for her endless hours of proofing; and Kalan Powers, who assisted with research, developing solutions, accuracy checking, and typing.

My students who provide continued opportunities for me to learn and are always ready to give me honest and helpful feedback.

Karen Schoenebeck, author

CHAPTER 1

INTRODUCTION TO INTERPRETATION AND ANALYSIS

PURPOSE: **Chapter 1** introduces the range and magnitude of amounts reported on financial statements of well-known companies. Trend analysis and common-size statements are introduced. An understanding is developed for the information provided by ratios and whether an increasing or decreasing trend is usually preferred.

QUESTION: **For major corporations, are sales usually reported in the range of millions, billions, or trillions?** Read this chapter to find the answer.

FEATURED CORPORATIONS

AT&T Corporation (T NYSE) is still the #1 long-distance company in the United States, but competition has driven rates down. AT&T provides services in voice, data, and video telecommunications, including cellular telephone and Internet services. They provide these services to businesses, consumers, and government agencies. www.att.com

Best Buy Company, Inc. (BBY NYSE) is the #1 consumer electronics retailer, staying ahead of competitors Circuit City and CompUSA. It sells home office products, consumer electronics, entertainment software, and major appliances through retail stores under the names of Best Buy, Musicland, Sam Goody, Suncoast, Media Play, and On Cue. www.bestbuy.com

Circuit City, Inc. (CC NYSE) is the #2 retailer of consumer electronics (behind Best Buy) with more than 620 stores that are primarily superstores selling brand-name consumer electronics, personal computers, and entertainment software. The company is revamping its superstores in favor of more profitable items such as home office products, rather than the less profitable appliances. Circuit City is one of the eleven companies considered "great" by Jim Collins. www.circuitcity.com

Citigroup Inc. (C NYSE) is the world's second-largest financial services firm, a leading credit card issuer, and the first United States bank with more than $1 trillion in assets. Citigroup offers banking, asset management, insurance, and investment banking through more than 2,600 locations in the United States and 3,000 offices in 100 other countries. Subsidiaries include Salomon Smith Barney, Travelers Life and Annuity, CitiFinancial, and Primerica Financial Services. Citigroup is also a leader in online financial services. www.citigroup.com

Dell (DELL Nasdaq) is the world's #1 direct-sale computer vendor and is competing with Hewlett-Packard for the worldwide PC title. In addition to a full line of desktop and notebook computers designed for consumers, Dell offers network servers, workstations, storage systems, and Ethernet switches for enterprise customers. Dell's growing services unit provides systems integration, support, and training. www.dell.com

Disney Company, The Walt (DIS NYSE) is the #2 media conglomerate in the world behind AOL Time Warner. Disney owns the ABC television network, 10 broadcast TV stations, and more than 60 radio stations. It also has stakes in several cable channels such as ESPN (80%) and A&E Television Networks (38%). Walt Disney Studios produces films through Touchstone, Hollywood Pictures, and Miramax. Walt Disney Parks and Resorts (Walt Disney World and Disneyland) are the most popular resorts in North America. disney.go.com

Ford Motor Company (F NYSE) began a manufacturing revolution in the 1900s with its mass production assembly lines. Now the company is the world's largest pickup truck maker and the #2 producer of vehicles behind General Motors. Vehicles are produced under the names of Ford, Jaguar, Lincoln, Mercury, Volvo, and Aston Martin. Ford has a controlling interest in Mazda and has purchased BMW's Land Rover SUV operations. It also owns the #1 auto finance company, Ford Motor Credit, and Hertz, the world's #1 car-rental firm. The Ford family owns about 40% of the company's voting stock. www.ford.com

Gap Inc., The (GPS NYSE) operates approximately 4,200 clothing stores including casual styles at The Gap, GapKids, and BabyGap, fast-growing budget Old Navy, and the chic Banana Republic. All Gap clothing is private-label merchandise made specifically for the company. From the design board to store displays, the company controls all aspects of its trademark casual look. The founding Fisher family owns about a third of the company. www.gap.com

General Motors Corporation (GM NYSE) is the world's #1 maker of cars and trucks, with brands such as Buick, Cadillac, Chevrolet, GMC, Pontiac, Saab, and Saturn. It also designs and manufactures locomotives (GM Locomotive) and heavy-duty transmissions (Allison Transmission). Other nonautomotive operations include DirecTV (Hughes Electronics) and subsidiary GMAC provides financing. www.gm.com

Harley-Davidson Corporation (HDI NYSE) is the nation's #1 seller of heavyweight motorcycles and the only major maker of domestic motorcycles. The company offers 24 models of touring and custom Harleys through a worldwide network of more than 1,350 dealers. Harley models include the Electra Glide, the Sportster, and the Fat Boy. The company also makes motorcycles under the Buell nameplate. Besides its bikes, Harley-Davidson sells attitude -- goods licensed with the company name include a line of clothing and accessories. www.harley-davidson.com

Hewlett-Packard Company (HPQ NYSE) is a provider of computing and imaging solutions for business and home. The company provides enterprise and consumer customers a full range of high-tech products, including personal computers, servers, storage products, printers, software, and computer-related services. CEO Carly Fiorina lead the largest deal in tech sector history -- the acquisition of Compaq Computer -- in a stock transaction valued at approximately $19 billion. www.hp.com

Home Depot Inc., The (HD NYSE) is the world's largest home improvement chain and second-largest retailer after Wal-Mart. It owns and operates 1,500 do-it-yourself warehouse retail stores in the United States, Canada, and Latin America. These stores offer building materials, home improvement products, and related furnishings. www.homedepot.com

Intel Corporation (INTC Nasdaq) is the largest producer of semiconductors in the world currently possessing 80% of the market share. Intel's most notable products include its Pentium and Celeron microprocessors. Intel also makes flash memories and is #1 globally in this market. Dell is the company's largest customer. www.intel.com

International Business Machines Corporation (IBM NYSE) is the largest provider of computer hardware in the world. It is among the leaders in almost every market in which it competes, including mainframe and servers, storage systems, desktop and notebook PCs, and peripherals. The company's service arm is the largest in the world. IBM is also one of the largest providers of both software (behind Microsoft) and semiconductors. www.ibm.com

Johnson & Johnson (JNJ NYSE) is one of the world's largest, most diversified health care product makers and offers products for the consumer, pharmaceutical, and professional markets. Brands include Tylenol, Band-Aid, Reach, Neutrogena, and ACUVUE contact lenses. www.jnj.com

LSI Logic Corporation (LSI NYSE) is a leading supplier in communications chips for broadband, data networking, and wireless applications. LSI Logic was a pioneer of system-on-a-chip (SOC) devices, which combine elements of an electronic system -- especially a microprocessor, memory, and logic -- onto a single chip. LSI Logic's top customers include Sony, Hewlett-Packard, IBM, and Sun Microsystems. www.lsilogic.com

Microsoft Corporation (MSFT Nasdaq) is the world's #1 software company that develops, manufactures, licenses, and supports a variety of products and services, including its Windows operating systems and Office software suite. The company has expanded into markets such as video game consoles, interactive television, and Internet access. It is also targeting services for growth, looking to transform its software applications into Web-based services for enterprises and consumers. Microsoft has reached a tentative settlement to end an ongoing antitrust investigation, agreeing to uniformly license its operating systems and allow manufacturers to include competing software with Windows. www.microsoft.com

Oracle Corporation (ORCL Nasdaq) is a leading provider of systems software, offering a variety of business applications that includes software for data warehousing, customer relationship management, and supply chain management. Oracle's software runs on a broad range of computers including mainframes, workstations, desktops, laptops, and handheld devices. Oracle also provides consulting, support, and training services. www.oracle.com

Royal Caribbean Cruises Ltd. (RCL NYSE) is the world's second-largest cruise line (behind Carnival) providing cruises in Alaska, the Caribbean, and Europe on 25 different cruise ships. The firm's two cruise brands, Celebrity Cruises and Royal Caribbean International, carry over two million passengers a year to about 200 destinations. www.rccl.com

SBC Communications (SBC NYSE) is the #2 local telephone company after Verizon, offering wireline and wireless telecommunications services and equipment, directory advertising, electronic security services, and cable television services. SBC has 60 million phone lines with its biggest markets in California (Pacific Bell), Texas (Southwestern Bell), and Illinois (Ameritech). The company has combined its domestic wireless operations with those of BellSouth to form #2 Cingular Wireless (after Verizon Wireless) with more than 22 million subscribers in 38 states. Other services include long-distance and Internet access. www.sbc.com

Sun Microsystems (SUNW Nasdaq) is the leading maker of UNIX-based servers used to power corporate computer networks and Web sites. It also makes workstation computers and a widening range of disk- and tape-based storage systems. Unlike most hardware vendors, Sun makes computers that use its own chips (SPARC) and operating system (Solaris). Its software portfolio includes application server, office productivity, and network management applications. Sun also created the JAVA programming language that can run the same code on nearly any computer platform and is thus widely used on the Internet. www.sun.com

Wal-Mart Stores, Inc. (WMT NYSE) is the largest retailer in the world with about 4,600 stores. Its sales are greater than Sears, Target, and Kroger combined. Its stores include Wal-Mart discount stores, Wal-Mart Supercenters, and Sam's Club membership-only warehouse stores. Most of its stores are in the United States, but Wal-Mart is also the #1 retailer in Canada and Mexico. Wal-Mart also has operations in South America, Asia, and Europe. Wal-Mart was rated #1 on the 2002 Fortune 500 list. www.walmartstores.com

WorldCom Group (WCOEQ OTC) operates one of the world's leading communications networks that span six continents. However, for the first 3 months of 2002, revenues fell 2% due to consumers using more wireless and e-mail services and fewer wireline services resulting in a less favorable sales mix. Later in 2002, inquiries into WorldCom's accounting practices led to the departure of the company's CEO and CFO and the filing of fraud charges by the SEC. In 2003, WorldCom filed the largest bankruptcy in corporate history and plans to reduce the workforce by 5,000 positions, primarily from corporate and administrative functions. www.worldcom.com

Wrigley (Wm) Jr. Company (WWW NYSE) is the world's #1 maker of chewing gum. Its products include such popular brands as Doublemint, Extra, Freedent, Juicy Fruit, and Spearmint. The Wrigley and Offield families control about 60% of the voting shares. CEO Bill Wrigley, Jr., represents the fourth generation of management. www.wrigley.com

----
Numerous sources including *Hoover's Company Capsules*, Hoover's, Inc., 2003.

EXAMINING TOTAL ASSETS
Comparing Companies

Purpose: · Examine the range and magnitude of total assets.
· Solve for unknowns in the accounting equation.
· Identify information provided by the balance sheet.

1.   The accounting equation is **Assets** = _____ + _____.

2.   For each company below, solve for the missing item in the accounting equation.

($ in millions)	GAP INC. 02/02/02	GENERAL MOTORS (GM) 12/31/02	ROYAL CARIBBEAN 12/31/02	ORACLE 5/31/02
Assets	$7,683	$	$10,538	$
Liabilities	$	$365,057	$ 6,504	$4,683
Stockholders' equity	$3,010	$ 6,814	$	$6,117

3.   Companies come in a wide range of sizes. One measure of size is total assets. To put the size of companies into perspective, examine the range and magnitude of the total asset values reported above. Note that all of the amounts reported above are in millions and, therefore, are missing the final (**three / six / nine**) zeros.

_____ is the *largest* company above, reporting total assets of

$_____ billion, _____ million, _____ thousand.

_____ is the *smallest* company above, reporting total assets of

$_____ billion, _____ million, _____ thousand.

4.   The corporations relying more on debt (than equity) to finance assets are
(**Gap Inc. / GM / Royal Caribbean Cruises / Oracle**).

5.   *Identify* the information provided by the balance sheet for decision makers.

6.   Examine the financial information above and *comment* on one item that you find interesting.

EXAMINING ASSETS
Comparing Companies

Purpose: · Examine asset components.
· Solve for unknown asset components.
· Understand assets are recorded at historical cost.

1. For each company below, solve for the missing asset item.

($ in millions)	DELL 2/01/02	IBM 12/31/02	Sun Microsystems 6/30/02
Current assets	$7,877	$41,652	$
Property, plant, and equipment, net	826	$	2,453
Other assets	4,832	40,392	6,292
Total assets	$	$96,484	$16,522

2. The company with the greatest dollar amount of current assets is (**Dell / IBM / Sun Microsystems / can't tell**). Would you expect this result? (**Yes / No**) *Explain* why or why not.

3. For all three companies, the largest asset account is (**current / PPE / other**) assets.
List at least three current asset accounts.

4. The company that has property, plant, and equipment (PPE) with the *greatest current market value* is (**Dell / IBM / Sun Microsystems / can't tell**). *Explain* your response.

5. Examine the financial information above and *comment* on one item that you find interesting.

6. These corporations are all in the (**bio-tech / computer / telecommunications**) industry.

Activity 3   **EXAMINING HOW ASSETS ARE FINANCED**
Comparing Companies

Purpose: · Solve for unknown liability and stockholders' equity components.
               · Determine the dominant method of financing assets.

1.   For each company below, solve for the missing liability or stockholders' equity item.

($ in millions)	DELL 02/01/02	IBM 12/31/02	MICROSOFT 6/30/02
Current liabilities	$ 7,519	$34,550	$15,466
Long-term liabilities	1,322	$	-0-
Contributed capital	5,605	14,858	$
Retained earnings	$	31,555	20,533
Other stockholders' equity	(2,275)	(23,631)	-0-
Total liabilities & stockholders' equity	$13,535	$96,484	$67,646

2.   A company has the choice of financing corporate assets with either debt (liabilities) or equity. For each corporation, compute total liabilities and total stockholders' equity. Record your results below (in millions).

     Total liabilities: $ _____ $ _____ $ _____

     Total stockholders' equity: $ _____ $ _____ $ _____

3.   The company relying more on debt (than equity) to finance assets is **(Dell / IBM / Microsoft).**

4.   IBM reports total assets of
     $(_____ **billion,** _____ **million,** _____ **thousand / can't tell**).

5.   Examine *long-term liabilities* and comment on one item of significance.

6.   Examine r*etained earnings* for Microsoft and comment on what this amount indicates.

7.   Identify one advantage of financing assets with common stock rather than with debt.

EXAMINING NET SALES
Comparing Companies

Purpose: · Examine the range and magnitude of net sales revenue.
· Solve for unknown income statement components.
· Identify information provided by the income statement.

1.   For each company below, solve for the missing item in the income statement.

($ in millions)	MICROSOFT fye 6/30/02	Royal Caribbean Cruises fye 12/31/01	WAL-MART fye 1/31/02	WALT DISNEY fye 9/30/02
Net sales revenue	$28,365	$	$219,812	$
Total expenses	20,536	3,083	$	24,093
Net income	$	$ 351	$ 6,671	$ 1,236

2.   Companies come in a wide range of sizes. One measure of size is net sales revenue. To put the size of companies into perspective, examine the range and magnitude of the net sales values reported above. Note that all of the amounts reported above are in millions and, therefore, are missing the final six zeros.

_____ is the *largest* company above, reporting *net sales revenue* of

$_____ billion, _____ million, _____ thousand.

3.   _____ is the *most profitable* company above, reporting *net income* of

$_____ billion, _____ million, _____ thousand.

4.   Do greater net sales revenue always result in greater net income? (**Yes / No**)

5.   The most profitable company measured by *net income as a percentage of sales* (Net income / Net sales) is (**Microsoft / Royal Caribbean / Wal-Mart / Walt Disney**).

6.   *Identify* the information provided by the income statement for decision makers.

7.   Examine the financial information above and *comment* on one item that you find interesting.

8.   The largest retailer in the world is (**Microsoft / Royal Caribbean / Wal-Mart / Walt Disney**).

RATIO ANALYSIS
Current Ratio

Purpose:
- Understand the information provided by the current ratio.
- Identify the expected range and whether an increasing or decreasing trend is usually preferred.

The **current ratio** compares current assets to current liabilities. This ratio measures the ability to pay current debts. It is a measure of short-term liquidity.

$$\text{CURRENT RATIO} = \frac{\text{Current assets}}{\text{Current liabilities}}$$

($ in millions)	GAP INC. 02/02/02	GENERAL MOTORS (GM) 12/31/02	Royal Caribbean Cruises 12/31/02	ORACLE 5/31/02
Current assets	$3,136	$173,013	$ 448	$8,728
Current liabilities	$2,148	$ 71,033	$1,170	$3,960

1. For each company listed above, compute the current ratio. Record your results below.

   Current ratio: ___1.46___ _____ _____ _____

2. The current ratios computed above are primarily in the range
   (**less than 1 / 1 through 3 / 3 through 5 / 5 or more**).

3. The company that has the strongest short-term liquidity as measured by the current ratio is
   (**Gap Inc. / GM / Royal Caribbean Cruises / Oracle**).

4. For the current ratio, a(n) (**increasing / decreasing**) trend is generally considered favorable.

5. Current liabilities are usually paid off with current assets. The corporation *not* able to pay off all current liabilities at this time is (**Gap Inc. / GM / Royal Caribbean Cruises / Oracle**).

   Does this indicate the corporation is insolvent or unable to pay its bills? (**Yes / No**) *Explain.*

6. A low current ratio generally indicates a lack of short-term liquidity. In general, such a firm will be required to pay (**higher / lower**) interest rates when borrowing money.

RATIO ANALYSIS
Debt Ratio

Purpose: · Understand the information provided by the debt ratio.
                 · Identify the expected range and whether an increasing or decreasing trend is preferred.

The **debt ratio** compares total liabilities to total assets. This ratio measures the proportion of assets financed by debt. It is a measure of long-term solvency.

$$\text{DEBT RATIO} = \frac{\text{Total liabilities}}{\text{Total assets}}$$

($ in millions)	CITIGROUP 12/31/02	HEWLETT-PACKARD 10/31/02	JOHNSON & JOHNSON 12/31/02	WAL-MART 1/31/02
Assets	$1,097,190	$70,710	$40,556	$83,451
Liabilities	1,010,472	34,448	17,859	48,349
Stockholders' Equity	$ 86,718	$36,262	$22,697	$35,102

1. For each company listed above, compute the debt ratio. Record your results below.

   Debt ratio: _____**0.92**_____   _____   _____ _____ -

2. The debt ratios computed above are primarily in the range of (**less than 0.40 / 0.40 through 0.70 / 0.70 or more**).

3. _____% of Wal-Mart's assets are financed with debt.

4. (**Citigroup / Hewlett-Packard / Johnson & Johnson / Wal-Mart**) are relying more on debt to finance assets and have a debt ratio (**greater / less**) than 0.50.

5. Assume that the debt ratio indicates the degree of financial risk. (**Citigroup / Hewlett-Packard / Johnson & Johnson / Wal-Mart**) is assuming the most financial risk. For a company wanting to be lower risk and less dependent on debt, a(n) (**increasing / decreasing**) trend in the debt ratio is considered favorable. A company that has higher financial risk will, in general, be required to pay (**higher / lower**) interest rates when borrowing money.

6. *Explain* why a company with a greater debt ratio tends to be a higher financial risk.

7. Does a high debt ratio indicate a weak corporation? (**Yes / No**) *Explain* your answer.

Note: On March 17, 1997, the 30 companies comprising the Dow Jones Industrial Average (DJIA) changed. Hewlett-Packard, Johnson & Johnson, Travelers Group, and Wal-Mart replaced Bethlehem Steel, Texaco, Westinghouse Electric, and Woolworth's. In October of 1998, Travelers Group merged with Citicorp and became Citigroup.

RATIO ANALYSIS
Return on Sales (ROS) also referred to as *Net Profit Margin*

Purpose: · Understand the information provided by the return-on-sales ratio.
· Identify the expected range and whether an increasing or decreasing trend is preferred.

The **return-on-sales** ratio compares net income to net sales. It expresses net income as a % of sales revenue. This ratio calculates the proportion of every sales dollar resulting in profits. It is a measure of profitability.

$$\text{RETURN ON SALES} = \frac{\text{Net income}}{\text{Net sales}}$$

($ in millions)	WAL-MART fye 1/31/03	GENERAL MOTORS (GM) fye 12/31/02	HOME DEPOT fye 2/03/02	ORACLE fye 5/31/02
Net sales	$246,525	$186,763	$53,553	$9,673
Total expenses	238,486	185,027	50,509	7,449
Net income	$ 8,039	$ 1,736	$ 3,044	$2,224

1. For each company listed above, compute return on sales. Record your results below.

   Return on sales: _____0.0326_____   _____   _____   _____

2. The return-on-sales ratios computed above are primarily in the range
   (**less than 0.01 / 0.01 through 0.10 / 0.10 or more**).

3. General Motors has much greater sales than Oracle, but the return-on-sales ratio of General Motors is (**greater than / equal to / less than**) the return-on-sales ratio for Oracle. The return-on-sales ratio for Oracle indicates _____% of every sales dollar resulted in profits (net income), but for General Motors only _____% of every sales dollar resulted in profits.

4. For Wal-Mart, _____ cents of each sales dollar went to pay for all of the costs of running the business, leaving _____ cents of each sales dollar for profit.

5. For the return-on-sales ratio, a(n) (**increasing / decreasing**) trend is favorable and indicates increasing profitability. The corporation with the strongest return-on-sales ratio is (**Wal-Mart / GM / Home Depot / Oracle**). How can a company increase its ROS ratio?

6. Does a low return-on-sales ratio indicate a weak corporation? (**Yes / No**) *Explain* your answer.

7. Examine the financial information above and *comment* on one item that you find interesting.

RATIO ANALYSIS
Asset Turnover

Purpose: · Understand the information provided by the asset turnover ratio.
· Identify the expected range and whether an increasing or decreasing trend is preferred.

The **asset turnover** ratio compares net sales to total assets. This ratio evaluates how efficiently assets are used to produce net sales. It is one measure of sales volume. It is a measure of profitability.

$$\text{ASSET TURNOVER} = \frac{\text{Net sales}}{\text{Average total assets}}$$

($ in millions)	WAL-MART	GENERAL MOTORS (GM)	HOME DEPOT	ORACLE
Net sales	fye 1/31/03 $246,525	fye 12/31/02 $186,763	fye 2/03/02 $53,553	fye 5/31/02 $ 9,673
Total assets	1/31/02 $ 83,527	12/31/01 $323,969	1/28/01 $21,385	5/31/01 $11,030
Total assets	1/31/03 $ 94,685	12/31/02 $371,871	2/03/02 $26,394	5/31/02 $10,800

1. December 31, 2001 assets are the ending assets of (**2000 / 2001 / 2002**) and the beginning assets of (**2000 / 2001 / 2002**).

2. For each company listed above, compute the average total assets for the most recent fiscal year. Average total assets = [(beginning assets + ending assets) / 2]. Record your results below (in millions).

   Average total assets: $__**89,106**__ $_____ $_____ $_____

3. For each company listed above, compute the asset turnover ratio. Record your results below.

   Asset turnover ratio: ____**2.77**____   _____   _____   _____

4. The asset turnover ratios computed above are primarily in the range (**less than 1 / 1 through 3 / 3 or more**).

5. The corporation with the strongest asset turnover ratio is (**Wal-Mart / GM / Home Depot / Oracle**).

6. For the asset turnover ratio, a(n) (**increasing / decreasing**) trend is favorable and indicates effective use of assets to produce net sales.

7. Home Depot makes profits by generating a large volume of sales on items with low prices. The asset turnover ratio is one measure of sales volume. Therefore, the asset turnover ratio for Home Depot is expected to be relatively (**high / low**).

8. *The 2002 Fortune 500 list* ranked (**Home Depot / GM / Wal-Mart / Oracle**) Number 1, indicating it is the largest corporation in the United States. *Hint*: Refer to Featured Corporations descriptions at the beginning of the chapter for the answer.

RATIO ANALYSIS
Return on Assets (ROA)

Purpose:
- Understand the information provided by the return-on-assets ratio.
- Identify the expected range and whether an increasing or decreasing trend is preferred.

The **return-on-assets** ratio compares net income to total assets. This ratio evaluates how effectively assets are used to produce profits (net income). This ratio incorporates both the return-on-sales ratio and the asset turnover ratio, and is the best measure of overall profitability.

$$\text{RETURN ON ASSETS} = \frac{\text{Net income + Interest expense}}{\text{Average total assets}}$$

$$\text{RETURN ON ASSETS} = \text{Return on sales x Asset turnover ratio}$$

($ in millions)	WAL-MART fye 1/31/03	GENERAL MOTORS (GM) fye 12/31/02	HOME DEPOT fye 2/03/02	ORACLE fye 5/31/02
Return on sales	.0326	0.0093	.0568	0.2299
Asset turnover	2.77	0.54	2.24	0.89

1. For each company listed above, compute the return-on-assets ratio. Record your results below.

   Return on assets: __0.0903__   _____   _____   _____

2. The return-on-assets ratios computed above are primarily in the range of
   (**less than 0.05 / 0.05 through 0.20 / 0.20 or more**).

3. The return-on-assets ratio for Wal-Mart indicates that approximately _____ cents of every dollar invested in assets resulted in profits.

4. The corporation with the strongest return-on-assets ratio is (**Gap Inc / GM / Royal Caribbean/ Oracle**).

5. For the return-on-assets ratio, a(n) (**increasing / decreasing**) trend is favorable and indicates increasing profitability.

6. Refer to the ratio information above.
   (**Return on sales / Asset turnover**) contributed more to the profitability of Home Depot.
   (**Return on sales / Asset turnover**) contributed more to the profitability of Oracle.

7. Examine the financial information above and *comment* on one item that you find interesting.

8. (**Gap Inc / GM / Royal Caribbean / Oracle**) competes with Microsoft in the computer software industry.

Note: Activity 52 provides additional information on the return-on-assets ratio.

TEST YOUR UNDERSTANDING
A Review of Ratio Analysis

HARLEY-DAVIDSON, INC.

	For the fiscal year ended	12/31/02	12/31/01	12/31/00
(P/L/S)	Current ratio	2.087	2.326	2.610
(P/L/S)	Debt ratio	0.145	0.180	0.200
(P/L/S)	Return on sales	0.142	0.130	0.120
(P/L/S)	Return on assets	0.150	0.140	0.143

1. In the left-hand margin above, circle whether the ratio measures *(P)rofitability*, short-term *(L)iquidity* -- the ability to pay current debt, or long-term *(S)olvency* -- the ability to pay long-term debt.

2. For each short-term liquidity ratio above, circle the ratio indicating the greatest ability to pay current liabilities for the three years of information presented.

    This company appears to (**have / not have**) the ability to pay current debt.

3. For each long-term solvency ratio above, circle the ratio indicating the least amount of debt financing for the three years of information presented.

    This company relies more heavily on (**debt / equity**) to finance assets.

4. For each profitability ratio above, circle the ratio indicating the greatest profitability over the three years of information presented.

    The profitability of this company appears to be (**strong / weak**).

5. Refer to all of the ratio information presented above. This company appears to be (**strong / weak**). *Explain* your answer.

6. The ratio that measures the proportion of total assets financed with liabilities is
    (**Return on sales / Return on assets / the Current ratio / the Debt ratio**).

7. The ratio that measures the proportion of net sales resulting in profits is the
    (**Return on sales / Return on assets / the Current ratio / the Debt ratio**).

8. The ratio that measures how effectively assets are used to generate profits is the
    (**Return on sales / Return on assets / the Current ratio / the Debt ratio**).

9. A supplier extending credit to a company for 60 days would be most interested in examining the
    (**Return on sales / Return on assets / the Current ratio / the Debt ratio**).

TREND PERCENTAGES
Income Statement

Purpose: · Prepare a trend analysis and understand the information provided.

A **trend analysis** compares amounts from a more recent year to a base year. The base year is the earliest year being studied. The analysis measures the percentage of change from the base year.

1. Using the amounts listed below, complete the trend analysis by dividing each amount by the amount for the base year. Record the resulting *trend percentage* in the shaded area. Use 1999 as the base year.

Johnson & Johnson ($ in millions)	2002		2001		2000		BASE YEAR 1999	
Net sales	$36,298	132%	$33,004	120%	$29,139	106%	$27,471	100%
Total expenses	29,647		27,336		24,339		23,304	
Net income	$ 6,651		$ 5,668		$ 4,800		$ 4,167	

2. Net sales of Johnson & Johnson increased by 32% from 1999 to 2002, while total expenses increased

    by _____% during the same period.

3. When net sales increase, expenses would be expected to (**increase / stay the same / decrease**).

4. It is favorable when sales increase by 32% and expenses increase at a (**greater / lesser**) rate than 32%.

5. For Johnson & Johnson, (**revenues / expenses**) increased at a greater rate from 1999 to 2002.

    This is (**favorable / unfavorable**).

6. Assume Johnson & Johnson has a goal of increasing profits by 5% each year.

    Johnson & Johnson (**met / did not meet**) this goal.

7. It is easier to analyze Johnson & Johnson (**before / after**) preparing the trend analysis.

8. Examine the financial information above and *comment* on one item that you find interesting.

9. Johnson & Johnson competes within the (**beverage / computer / pharmaceuticals**) industry.

Activity 12

TREND PERCENTAGES
Balance Sheet

Purpose: · Prepare a trend analysis and understand the information provided.

A **trend analysis** compares amounts from a more recent year to a base year. The base year is the earliest year being studied. The analysis measures the percentage of change from the base year.

1. Using the amounts listed below, complete the trend analysis by dividing each amount by the amount for the base year. Record the resulting *trend percentage* in the shaded area. Use 1999 as the base year.

Circuit City ($ in millions)	2/28/02	2/28/01	2/29/00	BASE YEAR 2/28/99
Assets	$4,133 132%	$3,452 110%	$3,537 113%	$3,135 100%
Liabilities	1,573	1,195	1,483	1,309
Stockholders' equity	$2,560	$2,257	$2,054	$1,826

2. The assets of Circuit City increased by 32% from 2/28/99 to 2/28/02.

   Circuit City is (**growing / shrinking**).

3. For Circuit City, (**assets / liabilities**) increased at a greater rate from 2/28/99 to 2/28/02. This is an indication the corporation is relying (**more / less**) on debt to finance assets.

4. When the trend percentage is *greater than 100*, it indicates the amount is (**greater than / less than**) the base year amount. Liability amounts are greater than the base year on (**2-28-02 / 2-28-01 / 2-29-00**).

   When the trend percentage is *less than 100*, it indicates the amount is (**greater than / less than**) the base year amount. Liability amounts are less than the base year on (**2-28-02 / 2-28-01 / 2-29-00**).

5. The worst year financially for Circuit City was the fiscal year ending (**2-28-02 / 2-28-01 / 2-29-00 / 2-28-99**). *Explain* the reason for your response.

6. The best year financially for Circuit City was the fiscal year ending (**2-28-02 / 2-28-01 / 2-29-00 / 2-28-99**). *Explain* the reason for your response.

7. It is easier to analyze Circuit City (**before / after**) preparing the trend analysis.

Activity 13

COMMON-SIZE STATEMENT ANALYSIS
Income Statement

Purpose: · Prepare common-size statements and understand the information provided.

Common-size income statements compare all amounts to net sales. The analysis measures each item as a percentage of net sales.

1. For each company listed below, complete the common-size statements by dividing each item on the income statement by net sales. Record your results in the shaded area provided below.

($ in millions)	AT&T fye 12/31/02		WORLDCOM fye 12/31/01		SBC Communications fye 12/31/02	
Net sales	$ 37,827		$21,348		$43,138	
		100.0%		%		%
Total expenses	50,909		19,824		37,485	
		134.6%		%		%
Net income	$(13,082)		$ 1,524		$ 5,653	
		(34.6)%		%		%

2. (**AT&T / WorldCom / SBC Communications**) is the largest company above reporting net sales of

    $_____ billion, _____ million, _____ thousand.

3. The company reporting more expense than revenue is (**AT&T / WorldCom / SBC Communications**).

4. Return-on-sales ratio = Net income / Net sales.
    The return on sales for AT&T is _____ (decimal form) or _____ %.

5. In the common-size income statement, every amount is compared to or divided by
    _____ .

6. Based only on the information provided above, which company would be your choice of investment? (**AT&T / WorldCom / SBC Communications**) *Why?*

7. *Identify* additional information that would be helpful in determining your choice of investment.

8. Examine the financial information above and *comment* on one item that you find interesting.

9. The corporations listed above are all in the (**entertainment / retail / telecommunications**) industry.

10. Common-size statements are helpful when comparing companies of different size. (**True / False**)

COMMON-SIZE STATEMENT ANALYSIS
Balance Sheet

Purpose: · Prepare common-size statements and understand the information provided.

The **common-size balance sheet** compares all amounts to total assets. The analysis measures each item as a percentage of total assets.

1. For each corporation listed below, complete the common-size statements by dividing each item on the balance sheet by total assets. Record your results in the shaded area provided below.

($ in millions)	LSI LOGIC 12/31/01		FORD 12/31/01		INTEL 12/29/01	
Total liabilities	$2,146	46%	$268,757	%	$ 8,565	%
Contributed capital	2,909	63%	6,020	%	8,833	%
Retained earnings	(320)	(7)%	10,502	%	27,150	%
Other stockholders' equity	(110)	(2)%	(8,736)	%	(153)	%
Total liabilities & stockholders' equity	$4,625	100%	$276,543	%	$44,395	%

Note: The percentages may not sum to 100% due to rounding error.

2. **(LSI Logic / Ford / Intel)** assets are most heavily financed with *borrowed* amounts.

3. **(LSI Logic / Ford / Intel)** assets are most heavily financed with amounts *invested by shareholders*.

4. **(LSI Logic / Ford / Intel)** assets are most heavily financed with *past profits*.

5. Debt Ratio = Total liabilities / Total assets.
    The debt ratio for LSI Logic is _____ (decimal form) or _____%.

6. The corporation that appears to be assuming the most financial risk is **(LSI Logic / Ford / Intel)**.

7. On the common-size balance sheet, every amount is compared to or divided by total (**assets / liabilities / stockholders' equity**).

8. Examine the financial information above and *comment* on one item that you find interesting.

9. **(LSI Logic / Ford / Intel)** is the largest producer of semiconductors in the world, currently possessing 80% of the market share.

TEST YOUR UNDERSTANDING
A Review of Trend Percentages and Common-Size Statements

BEST BUY ($ in millions)	fye 3/02/2002	fye 3/03/2001	fye 2/26/2000	fye 2/27/1999
Net sales	$19,597 _____%	$15,327 _____%	$12,494 _____%	$10,065 100%
Net income	$ 570 _____%	$ 396 _____%	$ 347 _____%	$ 216 _____%

1. Using the amounts listed above for Best Buy, complete the trend percentages by dividing each amount by the amount for the base year. Record the resulting *trend percentage* in the shaded area. Use the fiscal year ending in 1999 as the base year.

2. Net sales of Best Buy increased by _____% from 1999 to 2002,

   while net income increased by _____% during the same period.

3. For Best Buy, (**revenues / expenses**) increased at a greater rate from 1999 to 2002.

   This is a(n) (**favorable / unfavorable**) sign.

Wrigley (Wm) Jr. ($ in millions)	12/31/02	12/31/01	12/31/00	12/31/99
Assets	$2,108 _____%	$1,778 _____%	$1,575 _____%	$1,548 _____%
Liabilities	586 _____%	502 _____%	442 _____%	409 _____%
Stockholders' equity	$1,522 _____%	$1,276 _____%	$1,133 _____%	$1,139 _____%

4. Using the amounts listed above for Wrigley, complete the trend percentages by dividing each amount by the amount for the base year. Record the resulting *trend percentage* in the shaded area. Use 12/31/99 as the base year.

5. Assets of Wrigley increased by _____ % from 12/31/99 to 12/31/02.
   Wrigley is (**growing / shrinking**).

6. For Wrigley, (**assets / liabilities**) increased at a greater rate from 12/31/99 to 12/31/02.
   This indicates the corporation is relying (**more / less**) on debt to finance assets.

7. In the common-size *income statement*, every amount is compared to or divided by _____.

8. In the common-size *balance sheet*, every amount is compared to or divided by _____.

CHAPTER 2

ANALYZING THE BALANCE SHEET

PURPOSE: Chapter 2 introduces strategies for analyzing the balance sheet and then applies those strategies. Classified balance sheets, trend analyses, and common-size statements are prepared and followed by questions that lead you through interpretation to understanding.

QUESTION: Does an increase in retained earnings indicate the company issued more stock, purchased more assets, or reported net income? Read this chapter for the answer.

FEATURED CORPORATIONS

Citigroup Inc. (C NYSE) is the world's second-largest financial services firm, a leading credit card issuer, and the first United States bank with more than $1 trillion in assets. Citigroup offers banking, asset management, insurance, and investment banking through more than 2,600 locations in the United States and 3,000 offices in 100 other countries. Subsidiaries include Salomon Smith Barney, Travelers Life and Annuity, CitiFinancial, and Primerica Financial Services. Citigroup is also a leader in online financial services. www.citigroup.com

The Coca-Cola Company (KO NYSE) was established in 1886 and is now the world's largest soft drink company operating in approximately 200 countries and commanding approximately 50% of the global soft-drink market. The firm, which does no bottling, sells about 300 drinks brands, including Coca-Cola, Sprite, Barq's, Minute Maid, and Dasani and Evian water. www.cocacola.com

IHOP Corporation (IHP NYSE) develops, operates, and franchises International House of Pancakes restaurants. In 2002, there were 1,028 IHOP restaurants located in 41 states and Canada. Over 90% of the restaurants are franchised. www.ihop.com

LSI Logic Corporation (LSI NYSE) is a leading supplier in communications chips for broadband, data networking, and wireless applications. LSI Logic was a pioneer of system-on-a-chip (SOC) devices, which combine elements of an electronic system -- especially a microprocessor, memory, and logic -- onto a single chip. LSI Logic's top customers include Sony, Hewlett-Packard, IBM, and Sun Microsystems. www.lsilogic.com

McDonald's Corporation (MCD NYSE) is the world's #1 fast-food chain, operating more than 30,000 restaurants in 121 countries worldwide. In addition to the familiar freestanding locations, McDonald's has mini-restaurants at locations within Wal-Mart and Chevron stores. In addition to the burger business, McDonald's owns the Donatos Pizza chain and the 650-unit Boston Market chain. Much of the new growth is in foreign markets that now generate over 60% of sales. www.mcdonalds.com

Nike, Inc. (NKE NYSE) is the world's #1 shoe company with a 40% market share in the United States athletic shoe market. Nike also sells Cole Haan dress and casual shoes and a line of athletic apparel and equipment. Nike sells its products throughout the US and in about 140 other countries. Chairman, CEO, and co-founder Phil Knight owns more than 80% of the firm. The swoosh logo that is recognized worldwide was designed by a college student for $35. www.nike.com

Outback Steakhouse, Inc. (OSSI Nasdaq) is one of the largest casual-dining steak house chains, with some 780 Outback Steakhouse restaurants (decorated with boomerangs, surfboards, and other Australian fare) in the United States and 21 other countries. Most of the restaurants are company-owned and feature steaks, prime rib, chicken, fish, and pasta at reasonable prices. It also has some 120 Carrabba's Italian Grills, 6 Fleming's Prime Steakhouses (upscale dining), 14 Euro-Asian style Roy's restaurants, and 13 Bonefish Grills. www.outback.com

Sears, Roebuck and Co. (S NYSE) is one of the United States top retailers operating 860 mall-based stores, 470 automotive and hardware stores, and 800 independently owned Sears stores in smaller communities. The stores promote the Sears brands of apparel, tools, and appliances—Crossroads, Craftsman, and Kenmore. Sears also provides home services under the Sears HomeCentral brand and is selling appliances and tools via the Internet. www.sears.com

Southwest Airlines Co. (LUV NYSE) has expanded its low-cost, no-frills approach to air travel throughout the US to service 60 cities in 30 states. Its approach to cutting costs includes ticketless travel on only Boeing 737s, which resulted in 30 straight profitable years. www.southwest.com

Starbucks Corporation (SBUX Nasdaq) is the leading specialty coffee retailer with 5,900 coffee shops positioned throughout 25 countries in office buildings, malls, airports, and other locations. In addition to coffee, Starbucks offers coffee beans, pastries, mugs, coffee makers, coffee grinders, and even coffee ice cream. The company also sells its beans to restaurants, businesses, airlines, and hotels, and it offers mail order and online catalogs. Starbucks has expanded into Frappuccino, a bottled coffee drink, jointly with PepsiCo. www.starbucks.com

Walgreen Company (WAG NYSE) is the nation's largest drugstore chain with more than 3,900 stores in 43 states and Puerto Rico. Prescription drugs account for almost 60% of sales; the remainder comes from general merchandise, over-the-counter medications, cosmetics, and groceries. Walgreen builds rather than buys stores, so it can pick prime, high-traffic locations. For added convenience, more than two-thirds of its stores offer drive-through pharmacies and almost all offer one-hour photo processing. www.walgreens.com

Yahoo! Inc. (YHOO Nasdaq) claims the top spot among Internet portals drawing some 220 million visitors each month. Its site features a search engine and directory to help users navigate the Web with 25 international sites in 13 languages. Yahoo! compiles content from news, financial information, and streaming media sources, and offers registered users personalized Web pages, e-mail, chat rooms, and message boards. Most sales come from advertising that the company does on the website. www.Yahoo.com

----

Numerous sources including *Hoover's Company Capsules*, Hoover's, Inc., 2003.

Activity 16   **STRATEGIES FOR ANALYZING THE BALANCE SHEET**

Purpose: · Develop strategies for analyzing the balance sheet.
                · Understand what an increase or a decrease in an account indicates.

OUTBACK STEAKHOUSE, INC.

($ in millions)	12/31/01	12/31/00	12/31/99	12/31/98
Current assets	$ 206	$ 182	$143	$123
Property, plant, and equipment, net	813	694	607	538
Other assets	218	147	102	57
TOTAL assets	$1,237	$1,023	$852	$718
Current liabilities	$ 190	$ 168	$131	$117
Long-term liabilities	106	47	28	52
Common stock	221	216	195	179
Retained earnings	762	638	501	381
Treasury stock	(42)	(46)	(3)	(11)
TOTAL liabilities and stockholders' equity	$1,237	$1,023	$852	$718

1.   Total Assets are (**increasing / decreasing**).This company appears to be (**growing / shrinking**).

2.   The Common Stock account is (**increasing / decreasing**). This indicates the company is (**issuing more stock / purchasing more assets / reporting net income**). Outback Steakhouse issued the greatest amount of common stock during (**2001 / 2000 / 1999**).

3.   Retained Earnings is (**increasing / decreasing**). This indicates the company is (**issuing more stock / purchasing more assets / reporting net income**). Assuming Outback Steakhouse issued no dividends, the most profitable year was (**2001 / 2000 / 1999**).

4.   Compute the Current Ratio (Current assets / Current liabilities) for each year and *comment* on what the results indicate.

5.   Compute the Debt Ratio (Total liabilities / Total assets) for each year and *comment* on what the results indicate.

6.   Develop a strategy to evaluate the balance sheet. Which line would you look at first? Second? Third? *Explain* why.

7.   Review the series of balance sheets presented above. Outback Steakhouse appears to report a (**strong / weak**) financial position. *Support* your response with at least two observations.

INTERPRETING A BALANCE SHEET
Assets

Purpose: · Understand the meaning of amounts on the balance sheet.

SEARS, ROEBUCK and CO.

($ in millions)			12/29/01	12/30/00	1/1/00	1/02/99
(Ca/Ppe/O)	Cash equivalents	(+ / -)	$ 1,064	$ 842	$ 729	$ 495
(Ca/Ppe/O)	Marketable securities	(+ / -)	-0-	-0-	-0-	-0-
(Ca/Ppe/O)	Receivables	(+ / -)	28,813	17,823	18,437	18,369
(Ca/Ppe/O)	Inventories	(+ / -)	4,912	5,618	5,069	4,816
(Ca/Ppe/O)	Other current assets	(+ / -)	1,316	4,511	4,432	5,591
(Ca/Ppe/O)	Property, plant, equipment (PPE)	(+ / -)	13,137	12,585	11,912	11,326
(Ca/Ppe/O)	Accumulated depreciation	(+ / -)	6,313	5,932	5,462	4,946
(Ca/Ppe/O)	Investments	(+ / -)	-0-	-0-	-0-	-0-
(Ca/Ppe/O)	Deferred income tax	(+ / -)	415	174	367	572
(Ca/Ppe/O)	Intangibles	(+ / -)	-0-	-0-	-0-	-0-
(Ca/Ppe/O)	Other assets	(+ / -)	973	1,278	1,470	1,452
	TOTAL assets		$44,317	$36,899	$36,954	$37,675

1.   The beginning balance of the <u>cash equivalents</u> account was $_____ million for the year ended 12/30/2000.

2.   The <u>receivables</u> account (**increased / decreased**) by $_____ million during the year ended 12/30/2000.

3.   More <u>inventory</u> was acquired than sold to customers during the fiscal year(s) ending (**12-29-01 / 12-30-00 / 1-1-00**).

4.   From 1/02/99 to 12/29/01, the <u>property, plant, and equipment</u> account (**increased / decreased**), indicating that Sears is (**purchasing / selling**) more property, plant, and equipment.

5.   Amounts reported for the property, plant, and equipment account represents the (**acquisition cost / current market value / book value / present value**).

6.   The company paid a total of $_____ million for property, plant, and equipment as of 12/30/00.

7.   The book value of the property, plant, and equipment totals $_____ million as of 12/30/00. Book value = Acquisition cost of PPE minus Accumulated depreciation = PPE, net

8.   Refer to the financial information above and *comment* on at least one item of interest.

PREPARING A CLASSIFIED BALANCE SHEET
Assets

Purpose: · Practice classifying account titles.
· Interpret parentheses and minus signs reported on the financial statements.
· Prepare a classified balance sheet using asset accounts.
· Understand the meaning of amounts on the balance sheet.

Use the information presented for Sears on the previous page to answer the following questions.

1.   To the left of each account title above, circle whether the account should be classified as a
    (Ca)   Current asset,
    (Ppe)   Property, plant, and equipment, or as an
    (O)   Other (long-term) asset.
    The asset accounts on the previous page are listed in (**alphabetical order / order of liquidity / no particular order**). Asset accounts (**will / will not**) always be listed in this general order. The (**current asset / PPE / other asset**) accounts include long-term assets. (*Hint*: Circle all that apply.)

2.   To the right of each account title above, circle whether the amount is (**+**) added or (**-**) subtracted to compute total assets.

3.   When preparing financial statements, use the following rules for placing parentheses:
    •   Accounts that are *typically* <u>added</u> to compute total assets use no parentheses when added, and parentheses when subtracted.
    •   Accounts that are *typically* <u>subtracted</u> to compute total assets use no parentheses when subtracted, and parentheses when added.
    •   Parentheses indicate the (**same as / opposite of**) typical.
    •   A minus sign may be used instead of the parentheses.

    For example: Accumulated depreciation is typically (**added / subtracted**) to compute total assets. There are no parentheses around the amount for accumulated depreciation. For accounts that are typically subtracted, no parentheses indicate to (**add / subtract**) the amount.

4.   Use the information presented for Sears on the previous page to prepare the classified balance sheet below.
    a. Sears reports (**2 / 3 / 4 / 5 / 6**) current asset accounts, (**2 / 3 / 4 / 5 / 6**) property, plant, and equipment accounts, and (**2 / 3 / 4 / 5 / 6**) other asset accounts.

    b. For each date reported, calculate total (1) current assets, (2) property, plant, and equipment, net (book value), and (3) other assets. Then enter the result in the chart below.

    c. For each date reported, make certain CA + PPE, net + Other = Total assets.

SEARS ($ in millions)	**12/29/01**	**12/30/00**	**1/1/00**	**1/02/99**
Current assets	$	$	$	$29,271
Property, plant and equipment, net				6,380
Other assets				2,024
TOTAL assets	$44,317	$36,899	$36,954	$37,675

INTERPRETING A BALANCE SHEET
Liabilities and Stockholders' Equity

Purpose: · Understand the meaning of amounts on the balance sheet.

SEARS, ROEBUCK and CO.

($ in millions)			12/29/01	12/30/00	1/1/00	1/02/99
(Cl/L/Cc/R/O)	Accounts payable	(+ / -)	$ 7,176	$ 7,336	$ 6,992	$ 6,732
(Cl/L/Cc/R/O)	Notes payable	(+ / -)	3,557	4,280	2,989	4,624
(Cl/L/Cc/R/O)	Current portion of long-term debt and capital leases	(+ / -)	3,157	2,560	2,165	1,414
(Cl/L/Cc/R/O)	Unearned revenue	(+ / -)	1,136	1,058	971	928
(Cl/L/Cc/R/O)	Other current liabilities	(+ / -)	558	562	584	524
(Cl/L/Cc/R/O)	Long-term debt and lease obligations	(+ / -)	18,921	11,020	12,884	13,631
(Cl/L/Cc/R/O)	Postretirement benefits	(+ / -)	1,732	1,951	2,180	2,346
(Cl/L/Cc/R/O)	Deferred charges/income	(+ / -)	-0-	-0-	-0-	-0-
(Cl/L/Cc/R/O)	Minority interest/other LT liabilities	(+ / -)	1,961	1,363	1,350	1,410
(Cl/L/Cc/R/O)	Preferred stock	(+ / -)	-0-	-0-	-0-	-0-
(Cl/L/Cc/R/O)	Common stock, par	(+ / -)	323	323	323	323
(Cl/L/Cc/R/O)	Additional paid-in capital	(+ / -)	3,500	3,538	3,554	3,583
(Cl/L/Cc/R/O)	Retained earnings	(+ / -)	7,413	6,979	5,952	4,848
(Cl/L/Cc/R/O)	Treasury stock	(+ / -)	4,223	3,726	2,569	2,089
(Cl/L/Cc/R/O)	Other equities	(+ / -)	(894)	(345)	(421)	(599)
TOTAL liabilities and stockholders' equity			$44,317	$36,899	$36,954	$37,675

Use the information in the classified balance sheet above to answer the following questions.

1. The beginning balance of the <u>accounts payable</u> account was $_____ million for the year ended 12/30/2000.

2. The <u>notes payable</u> account (**increased / decreased**) by $_____ million during the year ended 12/30/2000.

3. As of 12/30/00 shareholders have contributed a total of $_____ million to this corporation.

4. The par value of the common stock is 75 cents per share. Approximately _____ million shares remain issued on 12/30/2000.

5. Assuming no dividends were issued, a total of $_____ million was reported for net income during the year ended 12/30/2000.

6. More <u>long-term debt and lease obligations</u> were borrowed than paid back during the year ended (**12-29-01 / 12-30-00 / 1-1-00**). The net amount borrowed that year totaled $_____ million.

PREPARING A CLASSIFIED BALANCE SHEET
Liabilities and Stockholders' Equity

Purpose: · Practice classifying account titles.
· Interpret parentheses and minus signs reported on the financial statements.
· Prepare a classified balance sheet using liabilities and stockholders' equity accounts.
· Understand the meaning of amounts on the balance sheet.

Use the information presented for Sears on the previous page to answer the following questions.

1. To the left of each account title on the previous page, circle the classification of the account as
    (Cl)   Current liability,
    (L)   Long-term liability,
    (Cc)   Contributed capital,
    (R)   Retained earnings, or
    (O)   Treasury stock and *other* stockholders' equity accounts.

2. To the right of each account title on the previous page, circle whether the amount is **(+)** added or **(-)** subtracted to compute total liabilities and stockholders' equity.

3. When preparing financial statements, use the following rules for placing parentheses:
    * Accounts that are *typically* <u>added</u> to compute total liabilities and stockholders' equity use no parentheses when added, and parentheses when subtracted.
    * Accounts that are *typically* <u>subtracted</u> to compute total liabilities and stockholders' equity use no parentheses when subtracted, and parentheses when added.
    * Parentheses indicate the (**same as / opposite of**) typical.
    * A minus sign may be used instead of the parentheses.

    For example: Treasury Stock is typically (**added / subtracted**) to compute total liabilities and stockholders' equity. There are no parentheses around the amount for the treasury stock account. For accounts that are typically subtracted, no sign indicates to (**add / subtract**) the amount.   Note: Treasury stock is common stock bought back by the issuing corporation with the intent to reissue at a later date. It is a contra-stockholders' equity account.

4. Prepare the following classified balance sheet using the information from the previous page. When completed, make certain CL + LTL + CC + RE + Other = Total liabilities and stockholders' equity.

SEARS ($ in millions)	12/29/01	12/30/00	1/1/00	1/02/99
Current liabilities	$	$	$	$
Long-term liabilities				
Contributed capital				
Retained earnings				
Treasury stock and other stockholders' equity				
TOTAL liabilities and stockholders' equity	$44,317	$36,899	$36,954	$37,675

5. Sears is relying most heavily on (**debt / contributed capital / retained earnings**) to finance assets.

6. *Contributed capital* amounts represent the (**amount paid-in / market / book / present**) value.

Activity 21   **TREND PERCENTAGES**

Purpose: · Prepare a trend analysis and understand the information provided.

TREND PERCENTAGES compare amounts from a more recent year to a base year. The base year is the earliest year being studied. The analysis measures the percentage of change from the base year.

1. Using the amounts listed below, complete the trend analysis by dividing each amount by the amount for the base year. Record the resulting *trend percentages* in the shaded area. Use 1998 as the base year.

LSI LOGIC ($ in millions)	12/31/01		12/31/00		12/31/99		BASE YEAR 12/31/98	
Current assets	$1,769	211	$2,072	248	$1,288	154	$ 837	100
Property, plant, and equipment, net	944		1,279		1,323		1,486	
Other assets	1,912		846		595		500	
TOTAL assets	$4,625	164	$4,197	149	$3,206	114	$2,823	100
Current liabilities	$ 510	85	$ 627	105	$ 475	79	$ 598	100
Long-term liabilities	1,635	233	1,072	153	875	125	701	100
Common stock	2,910		1,934		1,275		1,137	
Retained earnings	(320)	NA	673		435		368	
Other equities	(110)	NA	(109)	NA	146		19	
TOTAL L and SE	$4,625		$4,197		$3,206		$2,823	

2. <u>Total assets</u> of LSI Logic increased by 14% from 12/31/98 to <u>12/31/99</u>.
    Total assets of LSI Logic (**increased / decreased**) by _____% from 12/31/98 to <u>12/31/01</u>.

    LSI Logic is (**growing / shrinking**).

3. <u>Current liabilities</u> of LSI Logic decreased by 21% from 12/31/98 to <u>12/31/99</u>.
    Current liabilities of LSI Logic (**increased / decreased**) _____% from 12/31/98 to <u>12/31/01</u>.

4. When the trend analysis index is *greater than 100*, it indicates the amount is (**greater than / less than**) the (**previous / base**) year amount.

    When the trend analysis index is *less than 100*, it indicates the amount is (**greater than / less than**) the (**previous / base**) year amount.

5. LSI Logic reported the greatest increase in total assets during (**2001 / 2000 / 1999**). The annual rate of increase in total assets can be compared between companies.

   Assume less than 5% is low, 5-20% is moderate, and over 20% is high.

   The rate of annual asset growth for LSI Logic from <u>12/31/98 to 12/31/99</u> is (**low / moderate / high**).
   The rate of annual asset growth for LSI Logic from <u>12/31/00 to 12/31/01</u> is (**low / moderate / high**).

6. <u>Property, plant, and equipment, net</u> (**increased / decreased**) by _____% from 12/31/98 to 12/31/01. *Comment* on what this indicates.

7. <u>Long-term liabilities</u> (**increased / decreased**) by _____% from 12/31/98 to 12/31/01. *Comment* on what this indicates.

8. <u>Common stock</u> (**increased / decreased**) by _____% from 12/31/98 to 12/31/01. *Comment* on what this indicates.

9. <u>Retained earnings</u> (**increased / decreased**) by _____% from 12/31/98 to 12/31/01. *Comment* on what this indicates.

10. A $993 million net loss would most likely have occurred during (**2001 / 2000 / 1999**). This was determined by examining the decrease in the (**long-term liability / common stock / retained earnings**) account.

11. For LSI Logic, (**total assets / long-term liabilities**) increased at a greater rate from 12/31/98 to 12/31/01. This is an indication the corporation is relying (**more / less**) on long-term debt to finance assets.

    In general, this indicates the corporation is assuming a (**higher / lower**) financial risk than before.

12. Examine the financial information reported on the previous page and comment on at least one item that you find interesting.

13. A trend analysis compares amounts from a more recent year to a (**previous / base**) year.

14. A trend analysis is a helpful tool to further analyze a company. (**True / False**)

15. LSI Logic competes with Intel within the (**Internet / restaurant / semiconductor**) industry.

COMMON-SIZE STATEMENTS

Purpose: · Prepare common-size statements and understand the information provided.

The **COMMON-SIZE BALANCE SHEET** compares all amounts to total assets. The analysis measures each item as a percentage of total assets.

1.   For each corporation listed below, complete the common-size statements by dividing each item on the balance sheet by the amount of total assets. Record your results in the shaded area provided. When complete, make certain CA + PPE, net + Other = Total assets and CL + LTL + CS + RE + Other = Total L & SE.

($ in 000s)	IHOP 12/31/01		MCDONALD'S 12/31/01		STARBUCKS 9/29/02	
Current assets	$ 59,160	%	$ 1,819,300	8.1%	$ 847,538	%
Property, plant, and equipment, net	238,026	%	17,289,500	76.7%	1,265,756	%
Other assets	344,243	%	3,425,700	15.2%	179,442	%
TOTAL	$641,429 *	%	$22,534,500 *	100.0%	$2,292,736 *	%
Current liabilities	$ 44,529	%	$ 2,248,300	10.0%	$ 537,490	%
Long-term liabilities	284,470	%	10,297,000	45.7%	28,608	%
Common stock	80,046	%	2,108,600	9.3%	930,433	%
Retained earnings	233,920	%	18,608,300	82.6%	804,786	%
Other equities	(1,536)	%	(10,727,700)	(47.6)%	(8,581)	%
TOTAL	$641,429 *	%	$22,534,500 *	100.0%	$2,292,736 *	%

* Note: The percentages may not sum to 100% due to rounding error.

2.   The assets of (**IHOP / McDonald's / Starbucks**) are most heavily financed with *borrowed* amounts.

3.   The assets of (**IHOP / McDonald's / Starbucks**) are most heavily financed with amounts *invested by shareholders*.

4.   The assets of (**IHOP / McDonald's / Starbucks**) are most heavily financed with *past profits*.

5.   Debt Ratio = Total liabilities / Total assets.
     The debt ratio for McDonald's is _____% or _____ (decimal form).

6.   Common-size statements allow companies of different size to be more easily compared. (**T / F**)

7.   Examine the financial information of the three eating places above and *comment* on at least one item that you find interesting.

INDUSTRY NORMS
Eating Places

Purpose: · Compare industry norms with a company from within the industry.

Industry norms and ratios are reported by SIC code.
The SIC (standard industrial classification) code for eating places is 5812.
Dun & Bradstreet compiled the following balance sheet norms using information from over 1,000 eating establishments. Note: Refer to Activity 47 titled Researching Industry Norms for more information on SIC codes.

EATING PLACES

	Norm %	McDonald's %
Current assets	37.0	_____%
PPE	46.9	_____%
All other assets	16.1	_____%
TOTAL Assets	100.0	_____%
Current liabilities	30.7	_____%
Long-term liabilities	25.1	_____%
Stockholders' equity	44.2	_____%
TOTAL liabilities and stockholders' equity	100.0	_____%

Copyright 1996, Dun & Bradstreet, a company of The Dun & Bradstreet Corporation. Reprinted by permission.

1. Refer to the common-size percentages for McDonald's in Activity 22, the previous activity, to complete the above chart.

   a. The number of stockholders' equity accounts reported for McDonald's in Activity 22 total (**2 / 3 / 4 / 5**). Add the stockholders' equity common-size percentages together and enter the result in the chart above.

   b. On the remaining lines of the chart, record the common-size percentages for McDonald's from Activity 22.

2. Compare the industry norms to the asset information reported for McDonald's. *Comment* on your observations and what this may indicate.

3. Compare the industry norms to the liability and stockholders' equity information reported for McDonald's. *Comment* on your observations and what this may indicate.

Activity 24   **ANALYSIS of SOUTHWEST AIRLINES**

Purpose: · Understand and interpret amounts reported on the balance sheet.

SOUTHWEST AIRLINES CO.
BALANCE SHEET

($ in millions)	12/31/02	12/31/01	12/31/00	12/31/99
Cash	$1,815	$2,280	$ 523	$ 419
Receivables	174	72	138	75
Inventories	86	70	81	65
Other current assets	157	98	90	74
Property, plant, and equipment	9,456	8,902	7,968	6,849
Accumulated depreciation	2,810	2,456	2,148	1,841
Deposits and other assets	76	31	18	13
TOTAL assets	$8,954	$8,997	$6,670	$5,654
Accounts payable	$ 362	$ 505	$ 313	$ 267
Accrued expenses	529	548	500	430
Current portion of long-term debt	131	40	109	8
Other current liabilities	412	1,146	377	257
Long-term debt	1,553	1,327	761	872
Deferred income tax and other liabilities	1,545	1,417	1,158	984
Common stock par	777	767	508	505
Additional paid-in capital	136	50	104	350
Retained earnings	3,455	3,228	2,902	2,386
Treasury stock	-0-	-0-	62	903
Other stockholders' equity	54	(31)	-0-	-0-
TOTAL liabilities and stockholders' equity	$8,954	$8,997	$6,670	$5,654

Refer to the series of balance sheets presented for Southwest Airlines to answer the following questions.

1.   Total Assets have increased by $_____ million since 12/31/99, which is an increase of _____%. *Comment* on what this indicates.

2.   Southwest Airlines reported (**1 / 2 / 3 / 4**) contributed capital accounts. Total Contributed Capital has increased by $_____ million since 12/31/99, which is an increase of _____%. *Comment* on what this indicates.

3.   Retained Earnings has increased by $_____ million since 12/31/99, which is an increase of _____%. *Comment* on what this indicates.

4. Compute the <u>Book Value</u> of property, plant, and equipment for each year. Report $ in millions.

12/31/02 $_____; 12/31/01 $_____; 12/31/00 $_____; 12/31/99 $__5,008__

Comment on what the results indicate.

5. Southwest Airlines reports (**1 / 2 / 3 / 4**) current asset accounts and (**1 / 2 / 3 / 4**) current liability accounts. Compute the <u>Current Ratio</u> (Current assets / Current liabilities) for each year.

12/31/02 _____; 12/31/01 _____; 12/31/00 _____; 12/31/99 __0.658__

Comment on what the results indicate.

6. Southwest Airlines reports (**4 / 5 / 6 / 7**) liability accounts.
Compute the <u>Debt Ratio</u> (Total liabilities / Total assets) for each year.

12/31/02 _____; 12/31/01 _____; 12/31/00 _____; 12/31/99 __0.499__

Comment on what the results indicate.

7. Southwest distributed dividends of approximately $13.9 million during 2002.

Therefore, the approximate net income reported in 2002 is $_____ million.

8. Review the series of balance sheets presented for Southwest Airlines and *comment* on at least two items of significance.

9. Did the events of September 11, 2001, seem to have an effect on Southwest Airlines? (**Yes / No**)
Explain.

ANALYSIS of WALGREENS

Purpose: · Understand and interpret amounts reported on the balance sheet.

WALGREEN COMPANY
BALANCE SHEET

($ in millions)	08/31/02	08/31/01	08/31/00	08/31/99
Cash	$ 450	$ 17	$ 13	$ 142
Receivables	955	798	615	486
Inventory	3,645	3,483	2,831	2,463
Other current assets	117	96	92	131
Property, plant, and equipment	5,918	5,503	4,420	3,473
Accumulated depreciation	1,327	1,158	992	879
Other long-term assets	121	95	125	91
TOTAL assets	$9,879	$8,834	$7,104	$5,907
Accounts payable	$1,836	$1,547	$1,364	$1,130
Notes payable	-0-	441	-0-	-0-
Accrued expenses	1,018	937	848	730
Other current liabilities	101	87	92	64
Long-term debt	-0-	-0-	-0-	-0-
Deferred income tax	177	137	102	75
Other long-term liabilities	517	478	464	424
Common stock, par	80	79	79	78
Additional paid-in capital	748	597	367	259
Retained earnings	5,402	4,531	3,788	3,147
TOTAL liabilities and stockholders' equity	$9,879	$8,834	$7,104	$5,907

Refer to the series of balance sheets presented for Walgreen Company to answer the following questions.

1.   Total Assets have increased by $_____ million since 8/31/99, which is an increase of _____%. *Comment* on what this indicates.

2.   Walgreens reports (**1 / 2 / 3 / 4**) contributed capital accounts.
      Total Contributed Capital has increased by $_____ million since 8/31/99, which is an increase of _____%. *Comment* on what this indicates.

3.   Retained Earnings has increased by $_____ million since 8/31/99, which is an increase of _____%. *Comment* on what this indicates.

4.   Compute the <u>Book Value</u> of property, plant, and equipment for each year. Report $ in millions.

        8/31/02 $_____;   8/31/01 $_____;   8/31/00 $_____;   8/31/99 $__2,594__

        Comment on what the results indicate.

5.   Walgreens reports (**2 / 3 / 4 / 5**) current asset accounts and (**2 / 3 / 4 / 5**) current liability accounts. Compute the <u>Current Ratio</u> (Current assets / Current liabilities) for each year.

        8/31/02 _____;   8/31/01 _____;   8/31/00 _____;   8/31/99 __1.675__

        Comment on what the results indicate.

6.   Walgreens reports (**6 / 7 / 8 / 9**) liability accounts.
        Compute the <u>Debt Ratio</u> (Total liabilities / Total assets) for each year.

        8/31/02 _____;   8/31/01 _____;   8/31/00 _____;   8/31/99 __0.410__

        Comment on what the results indicate.

7.   Walgreens distributed dividends of approximately $134.6 million during 2000; $140.9 million during 2001; and $147.0 million during 2002.

        The approximate net income reported for the year ended 8/31/00 is $ ____775.6____ million.

        The approximate net income reported for the year ended 8/31/01 is $_____ million.

        The approximate net income reported for the year ended 8/31/02 is $_____ million.

8.   Review the series of balance sheets presented for Walgreens and *comment* on at least two items of significance.

9.   Sixty percent of Walgreen's sales come from (**prescription drugs / over-the-counter medications / general merchandise / one-hour photo processing**).

TEST YOUR UNDERSTANDING
Analyzing the Balance Sheet

Purpose: · Understand and interpret amounts reported on the balance sheet.

($ in millions)	Corp A 12/31/2002	Corp B 12/31/2001	Corp C 12/31/2002	Corp D 5/31/2002
Accounts payable	$ 91,426	$ 13	$ -0-	$ 504
Accrued expenses	-0-	236	4,686	768
Notes payable	-0-	-0-	2,475	425
Current portion of long-term debt	-0-	-0-	180	55
Total deposits	430,895	-0-	-0-	-0-
Other current liabilities	302,330	109	-0-	84
Long-term debt	126,927	-0-	2,701	626
Deferred income tax	-0-	-0-	399	142
Other long-term liabilities	58,894	24	2,260	-0-
Minority interest (long-term liability)	-0-	30	-0-	-0-
Preferred stock	1,400	-0-	-0-	-0-
Common stock, net	55	1	873	3
Additional paid-in capital	17,381	2,067	3,857	539
Retained earnings	81,403	(50)	24,506	3,495
Treasury stock	11,637	60	14,389	-0-
Other equities	(1,884)	10	(3,047)	(198)
TOTAL liabilities and stockholders' equity	$1,097,190	$ 2,379	$24,501	$6,443

1.   For each corporation, use the amounts above to prepare a <u>classified balance sheet</u>. Record the dollar amounts in the form on the next page. Reminder: Treasury stock is common stock bought back by the issuing corporation with the intent to reissue at a later date.

2.   On the next page, prepare a <u>common-size balance sheet</u> for each corporation using the amounts on the classified balance sheet you just prepared. Record the resulting percentages in the shaded area provided in the form.

3.   <u>Identify each corporation</u> by using the descriptions below and the financial information provided.

The **COCA-COLA COMPANY** was established in 1886, more than one hundred fifteen years ago, and is now the world's largest soft drink company operating in approximately 200 countries and commanding approximately 50% of the global soft-drink market. The firm, which does no bottling, sells about 300 drink brands, including Coca-Cola, Sprite, Barq's, Minute Maid, and Dasani and Evian water. Of the four corporations, Coca-Cola has paid out more to repurchase its own stock (treasury stock) than shareholders contributed for all of the shares previously issued. The company is primarily financed by past earnings.
The Coca-Cola Company must be Corp..(A / B / C / D).
(circle one)

NIKE INC. is the world's #1 shoe company with a 40% market share in the United States athletic shoe market. The company also sells a line of athletic apparel and equipment. Of the four corporations, Nike is primarily financed by past earnings and has no treasury stock.
Nike Inc. must be Corp..(A / B / C / D).
(circle one)

CITIGROUP INC. is the world's second-largest financial services firm, a leading credit card issuer, and the first United States bank with more than $1 trillion in assets. Citigroup offers banking, asset management, insurance, and investment banking through more than 2,600 locations in the United States and 3,000 offices in 100 other countries. Subsidiaries include Salomon Smith Barney, Travelers Life and Annuity, CitiFinancial, and Primerica Financial Services. Citigroup is also a leader in online financial services.

Citigroup Inc. must be Corp ....(A / B / C / D).

(circle one)

YAHOO! INC. is the top Internet portal drawing some 220 million visitors each month. Its site features a search engine and directory to help users navigate the Web with 25 international sites in 13 languages. Yahoo! compiles the news, financial information, streaming media sources, and offers registered users personalized Web pages, e-mail, chat rooms, and message boards. Most sales come from advertising on the website. Since going public, Yahoo!'s net losses exceed its net income. Despite the net losses, Yahoo! Inc. is able to attract significant investment capital. Of the four corporations, Yahoo! Inc. finances the greatest proportion of assets with contributed capital.

Yahoo! Inc. must be Corp ....(A / B / C / D).

(circle one)

CLASSIFIED BALANCE SHEETS

($ in millions)	CORP A	CORP B	CORP C	CORP D
TOTAL assets	$	$	$	$
	%	%	%	%
Total liabilities				
	%	%	%	%
Contributed capital				
	%	%	%	%
Retained earnings				
	%	%	%	%
Treasury stock and other equities				
	%	%	%	%
TOTAL L & SE	$1,097,190	$2,379	$24,501	$6,443
	100.0%	100.0%	100.0%	100.0%

4. Review the classified balance sheets above and *comment* on at least two items that you find interesting.

CHAPTER 3

ANALYZING THE INCOME STATEMENT

PURPOSE: Chapter 3 introduces strategies for analyzing the income statement and then applies those strategies. Multi-step income statements, trend analyses, and common-size statements are prepared and followed by questions that lead the student through interpretation to understanding.

QUESTION: If sales increase by 10%, would you also expect expenses to increase? Read this chapter to find the answer.

FEATURED CORPORATIONS

AMR Corporation (AMR NYSE) owns American Airlines and American Eagle. American Airlines is the United States' largest air carrier with a fleet of more than 800 jets serving approximately 160 destinations in the Americas, Europe, and the Pacific Rim (some through code-sharing). The carrier has recently expanded by acquiring TWA. In the airline industry slowdown that has followed September 11, 2001, American Airlines is working to reduce its capacity, its fleet, and its workforce. www.amrcorp.com

Anheuser-Busch Companies, Inc. (BUD NYSE) is the world's largest brewer and the largest beer producer in the United States with approximately half of the market share. It makes Budweiser, the nation's top-ranked beer, along with Bud Light, Michelob, and Busch. It is the largest recycler of aluminum cans in the world and one of the largest manufacturers of aluminum cans in the United States. It also operates amusement parks such as Busch Gardens and Sea World. www.anheuser-busch.com

AOL Time Warner, Inc. (AOL NYSE) is a dominant presence in most forms of media including AOL Internet services, cable, entertainment, television networks, music, and publishing. In the 2001 merger, America Online contributed the world's #1 online service, CompuServe, Netscape, and several interactive services, while Time Warner contributed film and TV, music, cable networks and systems, publishing, and professional sports. For 2002, even though revenues increased 10% to $41 billion the company reported a huge net loss, resulting from a $54 billion nonrecurring item for the impairment of goodwill. www.aoltimewarner.com

Best Buy Company, Inc. (BBY NYSE) is the #1 consumer electronics retailer, staying ahead of competitors Circuit City and CompUSA. It sells home office products, consumer electronics, entertainment software, and major appliances through retail stores under the names of Best Buy, Musicland, Sam Goody, Suncoast, Media Play, and On Cue. www.bestbuy.com

Boeing Company, The (BA NYSE) is the world's largest aerospace company, which develops and produces jet transports, military aircraft, and space and missile systems. It is the #1 manufacturer of commercial jets (currently losing market share to Airbus), the #3 defense contractor behind Lockheed Martin and Northrop Grumman, and one of the nation's leading exporters generating nearly half of its revenues from foreign sales. www.boeing.com

Carnival Corporation (CCL NYSE) is the world's #1 cruise operator with six cruise lines and 43 ships providing services to more than 2 million passengers each year. Carnival Cruise Lines offers affordable vacation packages primarily to Caribbean locations while their Holland America Line offers more luxury-oriented cruises to Europe, South America, and Alaska. www.carnivalcorp.com

Guess? Inc. (GES NYSE) was started as a designer jeans maker but now designs and markets trendy, upscale apparel and accessories for men, women, and children. Guess? sells its lines through more than 3,000 stores in North America and worldwide through more than 250 licensees. www.guess.com

Hasbro, Inc. (HAS NYSE) is the #2 toy maker in the US (after Mattel) and the producer of childhood favorites such as G.I. Joe, Play-Doh, Tonka toys, Nerf balls, and Playskool. Hasbro also offers an assortment of board games under its Milton Bradley and Parker Brothers brands. www.hasbro.com

Microsoft Corporation (MSFT Nasdaq) is the world's #1 software company that develops, manufactures, licenses, and supports a variety of products and services, including its Windows operating systems and Office software suite. The company has expanded into markets such as video game consoles, interactive television, and Internet access. It is also targeting services for growth, looking to transform its software applications into Web-based services for enterprises and consumers. Microsoft has reached a tentative settlement to end an ongoing antitrust investigation, agreeing to uniformly license its operating systems and allow manufacturers to include competing software with Windows. www.microsoft.com

PepsiCo, Inc. (PEP NYSE) is the world's #2 soft-drink maker and the world's #1 maker of snacks. Beverages include Pepsi (the #2 soft drink), Mountain Dew, Slice, Tropicana Juices (the world's leading juice manufacturer), Aquafina bottled water, All-Sport, Dole juices, and Lipton tea. PepsiCo also owns Frito-Lay, the world's #1 maker of snacks such as corn chips (Doritos, Fritos) and potato chips (Lay's, Ruffles, WOW!). www.pepsico.com

Southwest Airlines Co. (LUV NYSE) has expanded its low-cost, no-frills approach to air travel throughout the US to service 60 cities in 30 states. Its approach to cutting costs includes ticketless travel on only Boeing 737s, which resulted in 30 straight profitable years. www.southwest.com

UAL Corporation (UAL NYSE) operates United Airlines, the world's #2 air carrier (behind AMR's American Airlines). United Airlines flies 540 jets to more than 130 destinations in the United States and 27 other countries. At the beginning of 2003, UAL was still reorganizing under bankruptcy protection. The employees control 55% of the airline. www.united.com

Wal-Mart Stores, Inc. (WMT NYSE) is the largest retailer in the world with about 4,600 stores. Its sales are greater than Sears, Target, and Kroger combined. Its stores include Wal-Mart discount stores, Wal-Mart Supercenters that are a combination discount and grocery store, and Sam's Club membership-only warehouse stores. Most Wal-Mart stores are in the United States, but international expansion has made it the #1 retailer in Canada and Mexico. Wal-Mart also has operations in South America, Asia, and Europe. Wal-Mart was rated #1 on the 2002 Fortune 500 list. www.walmartstores.com

----

Numerous sources including *Hoover's Company Capsules*, Hoover's, Inc., 2003.

Activity 27   **STRATEGIES FOR ANALYZING THE INCOME STATEMENT**

Purpose: · Understand the relationship between the trend for net sales and the trend for other items on the income statement.
· Develop strategies for analyzing the income statement.

GUESS? INCORPORATED

($ in millions)	2001	2000	1999	1998
Net sales	$678	$779	$600	$472
Cost of goods sold	448	496	332	272
Gross margin	230	283	268	200
Operating expenses	206	240	174	143
Income from operations	24	43	94	57
Other gains (losses)	(13)	(13)	(7)	(14)
Income before income tax	11	30	87	43
Income tax expense	5	13	35	18
Net income	$ 6	$ 17	$ 52	$ 25

1. From 1998 to 2001, <u>revenues</u> have (**increased / decreased**), which indicates the company is (**staying competitive within its industry / successful at controlling costs / well managed**).

2. <u>Cost of goods sold</u> (COGS) is a(n) (**revenue / expense / asset / liability**) account that has (**increased / decreased**) from 1998 to 2001. The direction of change in this account is (**expected / unexpected**). *Explain* why.

3. From 1998 to 2001, <u>net income</u> has (**increased / decreased**), which indicates the company is (**not selling enough merchandise / not collecting amounts due from customers / incurring expenses at an increasingly greater rate than revenues**). The direction of change in this account is (**expected / unexpected**). *Explain* why.

4. Compute the <u>gross margin percentage</u> (Gross margin / Net sales) for each year.
    2001 _____%; 2000 _____%; 1999 _____%; 1998 _42.4_ %
    Comment on the results.

5. Compute the <u>return on sales ratio</u> (Net income / Net sales) for each year.
    2001 _____%; 2000 _____%; 1999 _____%; 1998 _5.30_ %
    Comment on the results.

6. Operationally, the best year was (**2001 / 2000 / 1999**) and the worst year was (**2001 / 2000 / 1999**). List as many items as you can to support your responses.

7. Develop a strategy to evaluate the income statement. Which line of the income statement would you look at first? Second? Third? *Explain* why.

Activity 28

PREPARING AND INTERPRETING
A MULTI-STEP INCOME STATEMENT

Purpose:
· Understand the meaning of amounts on the income statement.
· Practice classifying income statement account titles.
· Interpret parentheses and minus signs reported on the financial statements.
· Prepare a multi-step income statement.

PEPSICO, INC.

($ in millions)			2002	2001	2000
(R/E/O/T)	Net sales	**(+/-/E)**	$25,112	$23,512	$25,479
(R/E/O/T)	Cost of goods sold (COGS)	**(+/-/E)**	11,497	10,750	10,226
(R/E/O/T)	Selling, general, and administrative expenses (SGA)				
		(+/-/E)	8,523	8,189	11,104
(R/E/O/T)	Depreciation/amortization expense 147	**(+/-/E)**		138	165
(R/E/O/T)	Other operating expenses	**(+/-/E)**	224	387	184
(R/E/O/T)	Interest expense	**(+/-/E)**	178	219	272
(R/E/O/T)	Investment gains (losses)	**(+/-/E)**	316	227	215
(R/E/O/T)	Gain (loss) on the sale of assets	**(+/-/E)**	-0-	-0-	-0-
(R/E/O/T)	Income tax expense	**(+/-/E)**	1,555	1,367	1,218
	Net income		$ 3,313	$ 2,662	$ 2,543
	Outstanding shares (in millions)		# 1,789	# 1,763	# 1,748

Use the information presented for PepsiCo above to answer the following questions.

1. To the left of each account title, circle whether the account should be classified on a multi-step income statement as a(n): (**R**) operating revenue, (**E**) operating expense, (**O**) other gains (losses) or revenues (expenses), or as (**T**) income tax expense.

   Income statement accounts are listed in (**alphabetical order / order of relationship to the core business activity / no particular order**).

2. To the right of each account title, circle whether the amount is (**+**) added or (**-**) subtracted to compute net income. Circle (E) if the amount may be either added or subtracted to compute net income. *Hint*: There should be two (E)s circled above.

3. When preparing financial statements, use the following rules for placing parentheses.
   • Accounts that are *typically* <u>added</u> or that can <u>either</u> be added or subtracted to compute net income, use no parentheses when added and parentheses when subtracted.
   • Accounts that are typically <u>subtracted</u> to compute net income, use no parentheses when subtracted and parentheses when added.
   • Parentheses indicate (**to subtract / to add / to do the opposite of typical**).
   • A minus sign may be used instead of the parentheses.

   For example: Income tax expense is typically (**added / subtracted**) to arrive at net income. For accounts that are typically subtracted, no parentheses indicate to (**add / subtract**) the amount.

4. PepsiCo's core operating activity is to manufacture snack food and drinks, therefore, *operating revenues* are earned when _____ are sold. During 2002, *operating revenues* earned by PepsiCo total $_____ million and the cost of the products sold totals $_____ million.

5. Cost of goods sold *(COGS)* totaled $_____ million for 2000, $_____ million for 2001, and $_____ million for 2002. The beginning balance of COGS was $_____ million for 2000, $_____ million for 2001, and $_____ million for 2002.

6. Operating expenses are those expenses directly related to a company's core business activity. PepsiCo reported (**2 / 3 / 4**) operating expense accounts (other than COGS) that total $_____ million in 2002. (**COGS / Operating**) expenses are greatest in 2002, which is (**expected / unexpected**) for a manufacturing firm.

7. Other gains (losses) *also titled other revenues(expenses)* refer to *other* than operating revenues and expenses. Interest expense is a(n) (**financing / operating**) cost. Investment gains (losses) (**are / are not**) part of PepsiCo's core business activity. Gains (losses) on the sale of assets result from the sale of (**inventory / property, plant, and equipment**). Other gains (losses) accounts (other than income tax expense) total $_____ million in 2002.

8. Net sales *minus* (**income tax expense / operating expenses / other gains (losses) / COGS**) equals gross margin. For 2002, the amount reported for *gross margin* is $_____ million.

9. Gross margin *minus* (**income tax expense / operating expenses / other gains (losses) / COGS**) equals income from operations. For 2002, the amount reported for *income from operations* is $_____ million.

10. Income from operations *plus* or *minus* (**income tax expense / operating expenses / other gains (losses) / COGS**) equals *income before income tax.* For 2002, the amount reported for *income before income taxes* is $_____ million.

11. Income before income tax *minus* (**income tax expense / operating expenses / other gains (losses) / COGS**) equals *net income.* For 2002, the income tax rate was _____%.

12. Prepare the 2001 and 2000 multi-step income statements below using the amounts presented for PepsiCo on the previous page. The 2002 multi-step income statement has been completed to help with understanding.

PEPSICO ($ in millions)	2002	2001	2000
1. Net sales	$25,112	$	$
2. Cost of goods sold	11,497		
3. Gross margin	13,615		
4. Operating expenses	8,885		
5. Income from operations	4,730		
6. Other gains (losses)	138		
7. Income before income tax	4,868		
8. Income tax expense	1,555		
9. Net income (loss)	$ 3,313	$	$
10. Earnings per share (Net income / # shares outstanding)	$1.85 per share	$_____ per share	$_____ per share

Note: Record amounts in the shaded lines, then use those amounts to compute the subtotals in the nonshaded lines.

13. Earnings per share reports a(n) (**increasing** / decreasing) trend, which is considered (**favorable** / unfavorable).

ANALYZING THE INCOME STATEMENT
Using The Boeing Company

Purpose:
- Understand the relationship between the trend for sales and the trend for other items on the income statement.
- Use ratios to enhance understanding of amounts reported on the financial statements.
- Understand nonrecurring items may distort certain computations.

THE BOEING COMPANY

($ in millions)	2002	2001	2000	1999
Net sales	$54,069	$58,198	$51,321	$57,993
Cost of goods sold	45,499	48,778	43,712	51,320
Gross margin	8,570	9,420	7,609	6,673
Operating expenses:				
Selling, general, and administrative expenses	2,981	2,767	2,651	2,253
Research and development expense	1,639	1,936	1,441	1,341
Other operating expenses	82	821	459	(91)
	4,702	5,524	4,551	3,503
Income from operations	3,868	3,896	3,058	3,170
Other gains (losses):				
Interest expense	730	650	445	431
Other nonoperating income (expense)	42	318	386	585
	(688)	(332)	(59)	154
Income from continuing operations before income tax	3,180	3,564	2,999	3,324
Income tax expense	861	738	871	1,015
Income from continuing operations	2,319	2,826	2,128	2,309
Nonrecurring items	(1,827)	1	-0-	-0-
Net income	$ 492	$ 2,827	$ 2,128	$ 2,309
Outstanding shares (in millions)	# 799	# 816	# 860	# 917

1. Net sales (**increased / decreased**) from 1999 to 2002. This might indicate that the company is (**less competitive within its industry / selling long-term assets / distributing dividends**).

2. Cost of goods sold (**increased / decreased**) from 1999 to 2002. The direction of change in this account is (**expected / unexpected**). *Explain* why.

3. Compute the Gross Margin Percentage (Gross margin / Net sales) for each year.

    2002 _____%; 2001 _____%; 2000 _____%; 1999 __11.5__ %

    Comment on the results.

4. The greatest <u>operating expense</u> is (**cost of goods sold / selling, general, and administrative / research and development**). Is this expected? (**Yes / No**) *Explain* why.

5. <u>Selling, general, and administrative expenses</u> (**increased / decreased**) from 1999 to 2002. The direction of change in this account is (**expected / unexpected**). *Explain* why.

6. <u>Interest expense</u> (**increased / decreased**) from 1999 to 2002. *Identify* at least one event that would result in this trend.

7. <u>Nonrecurring items</u> are items that occur (**once / twice / continuously**) within the life of a company. For Boeing, a nonrecurring item that significantly impacted net income was reported in (**2002 / 2001 / 2000 / 1999**).

   The amount on the income statement that is the better predictor of future income is (**Income from continuing operations / Net income**). *Explain* why.

8. Compute <u>Return on Sales</u> (ROS) for each year using the following ratio formula: (Income from continuing operations / Net sales).

   2002 _____%; 2001 _____%; 2000 _____%; 1999 <u> 4.0 </u>%
   Comment on the results.

9. Compute <u>Earnings per Share</u> (EPS) for each year using the following ratio formula: (Income from continuing operations / Number of shares outstanding).

   2002 $_____ / share; 2001 $_____ / share; 2000 $_____ / share; 1999 $<u> 2.52 </u> / share
   Comment on the results.

10. Return on sales and earnings per share are ratios used by investors and creditors to predict future earnings. *Comment* on why "Income from continuing operations" is more appropriate than "Net income" for computing <u>Return on Sales</u> and <u>Earnings per Share</u> for Boeing.

11. Operationally, the best year was (**2002 / 2001 / 2000 / 1999**) and the worst year was (**2002 / 2001 / 2000 / 1999**). List as many items as you can to support your responses.

12. Boeing is the world's largest (**aerospace / retailer / financial services**) company. Its primary *commercial* jet competitor is (**Airbus / Lockheed Martin / Northrop Grumman**). (*Hint*: Refer to the Featured Corporation descriptions at the beginning of the chapter.)

TREND ANALYSIS
Using the Best Buy Company

Purpose: · Prepare a trend analysis and understand the information provided.

The **TREND ANALYSIS** compares amounts from a more recent year to a base year. The base year is the earliest year being studied. The analysis measures the percentage of change from the base year.

1. Using the amounts listed below, complete the trend analysis by dividing each amount by the amount for the base year. Record the resulting *index number* in the shaded area. Use the fiscal year ended 2/27/1999 as the base year. Some indexes have already been recorded to help with understanding.

BEST BUY ($ in millions)	fye 3/02/02		fye 3/03/01		fye 2/26/00		BASE YEAR fye 2/27/99	
Net sales	$19,597		$15,327		$12,494		$10,065	
		195		152		124		100
Cost of goods sold	15,167		12,268		10,101		8,250	
Gross margin	4,430		3,059		2,393		1,815	
Operating expenses	3,493		2,455		1,854		1,463	
Income from operations	937		604		539		352	
Other gains (losses)	(1)	Not applicable	38	Not applicable	24	Not applicable	0	100
Income before income tax	936		642		563		352	
		266		182		160		100
Income tax expense	366		246		216		136	
		269		181		159		100
Net income	$ 570		$ 396		$ 347		$ 216	
		264		183		161		100

Refer to the series of income statements and the trend analysis above for the Best Buy Company to answer the following questions.

2.

a. Net sales of Best Buy increased by 95% from fiscal year ended 2/27/99 to fiscal year ended 3/02/02. When net sales increase, expenses would be expected to (**increase / stay the same / decrease**).

b. It is favorable when sales increase by 95% and expenses increase at a (**greater / lesser**) rate than 95%.

c. For Best Buy, cost of goods sold increased by _____% from fiscal year ended 2/27/99 to fiscal year ended 3/02/02, which is a(n) (**favorable / unfavorable**) increase for this time period.

d. For Best Buy, operating expenses increased by _____% from fiscal year ended 2/27/99 to fiscal year ended 3/02/02, which is a(n) (**favorable / unfavorable**) increase for this time period.

e. For Best Buy, (**cost of goods sold / operating expenses**) is a more important cost to keep under control. *Explain* why.

3. For Best Buy, total (**revenues / expenses**) increased at a greater rate from fiscal year ended 2/27/99 to fiscal year ended 3/02/02. *Explain* how you can tell.

4. The annual rate of increase in net sales can be compared between companies.

   Assume less than 5% is low, 5-20% is moderate, and over 20% is a high rate of increase.

   On average, the rate of annual net sales growth for Best Buy would be considered (**low / moderate / high**).

5. Compute the <u>gross margin percentage</u> (Gross margin / Net sales) for each fiscal year ending on:

   3/02/02 _____%; 3/03/01 _____%; 2/26/00 _____%; 2/27/99 __18.03__ %

   Comment on the results.

6. Compute the <u>return on sales ratio</u> (Net income / Net sales) for each fiscal year ending on:

   3/02/02 _____%; 3/03/01 _____%; 2/26/00 _____%; 2/27/99 __2.15__ %

   Comment on the results.

7. Operationally, the best year was (**3-02-02 / 3-03-01 / 2-26-00 / 2-27-99**) and the worst year was (**3-02-02 / 3-03-01 / 2-26-00 / 2-27-99**). List as many items as you can to support your responses.

8. Review the financial information for Best Buy and *comment* on at least one item that you find of significance or of interest.

9. When the trend analysis index is greater than 100, it indicates the amount is greater than the (**base year / previous year**) amount.

10. It is easier to analyze Best Buy (**before / after**) preparing the trend analysis.

11. In 2003, Best Buy was the (**#1 / #2 / #3**) consumer electronics retailer, competing with Circuit City and CompUSA. (*Hint*: Refer to Featured Corporation descriptions at the beginning of the chapters.)

COMMON-SIZE STATEMENTS

Purpose: · Prepare common-size statements and understand the information provided.

The **COMMON-SIZE INCOME STATEMENT** compares all amounts to net sales. The analysis measures each item as a percentage of net sales.

1. For each corporation listed below, complete the common-size statements by dividing each item on the income statement by net sales. Record the resulting percentages in the shaded area provided. Some percentages have already been recorded to help with understanding.

($ in millions)	AMR (American Airlines) 2001		Southwest Airlines 2001		UAL (United Airlines) 2001	
Net sales	$18,963	%	$ 5,470	100.0%	$16,138	%
Cost of goods sold	14,889	%	3,630	66.4%	15,733	%
Gross margin	4,074	%	1,840	33.6%	405	%
Operating expenses	6,544	%	1,209	22.1%	4,176	%
Income from operations	(2,470)	%	631	11.5%	(3,771)	%
Other gains (losses)	(286)	%	+197	+3.6%	+414	%
Income before income tax	(2,756)	%	828	15.1%	(3,357)	%
Income tax expense	(994)	%	317	5.8%	(1,226)	%
Net income	$ (1,762)	%	$ 511	9.3%	$ (2,131)*	%

*excludes nonrecurring items

2. (**AMR / SW / UAL**) reported the greatest *net sales,* while (**AMR / SW / UAL**) reported the least net sales.

3. (**AMR / SW / UAL**) reported the greatest *gross margin percentage* ratio of _____ %.
   For the gross margin percentage ratio, a(n) (**increasing / decreasing**) trend is favorable.

4. (**AMR / SW / UAL**) reported the greatest *return-on-sales* ratio of _____ %.
   For the return-on-sales ratio, a(n) (**increasing / decreasing**) trend is favorable.

5. (**AMR / SW / UAL**) reported greater expenses incurred than revenues earned.

6. Review the financial information above and *comment* on at least two items that you find of significance or of interest.

INDUSTRY NORMS
Air Transportation, Scheduled

Purpose: · Compare industry norms to a company from within the industry.

Industry norms and ratios are reported by SIC code. The SIC (standard industrial classification) code for scheduled air transportation is 4512. Dun & Bradstreet compiled the following income statement norms using information from 100 airline companies.

Scheduled Air Transportation

	Norm %	Southwest Airlines %
Net sales	100.0	_____%
Gross margin	34.4	_____%
Net income	2.7	_____%

Copyright 1996, **Dun & Bradstreet, a company of The Dun & Bradstreet Corporation. Reprinted by permission.**

1. On the lines provided above, record the common-size amounts for Southwest Airlines from the previous page.

2. Compare the industry norms to the information reported for Southwest Airlines.
    Comment on your observations and what may account for the differences.

ANALYSIS of CARNIVAL CORPORATION

Purpose: · Understand and interpret amounts reported on the income statement.

CARNIVAL CORPORATION

Fiscal year ended ($ in millions)	11/30/02	11/30/01	11/30/00	11/30/99
Net sales	$ 4,368	$ 4,536	$ 3,779	$ 3,498
Cost of goods sold (COGS)	2,312	2,469	2,058	1,863
Gross margin	2,056	2,067	1,721	1,635
Selling, general, and administrative expenses (SGA)	612	619	487	447
Depreciation expense	382	372	288	244
Other operating expenses	20	184	(37)	(76)
Interest expense	111	121	41	47
Investment income (loss)	32	34	17	42
Other nonoperating income (loss)	(4)	109	8	29
Income tax expense	(57)	(12)	1	3
Net income	$ 1,016	$ 926	$ 966	*$ 1,041

* Income from continuing operations.

Refer to the series of income statements presented above to answer the following questions.

1. Since 11/30/1999, <u>net sales</u> have (**increased / decreased**) by $_____ million, which is a
   _____% change in sales. The annual rate of increase in net sales can be compared between
   companies.
   Assume less than 5% is low, 5-20% is moderate, and over 20% is a high rate of increase.
   Carnival's average annual rate of increase in net sales is considered (**low / moderate / high**).

2. <u>Depreciation expense</u> (**increased / decreased**) from 11/30/1999 to 11/30/2002, which MOST likely
   indicates that the company is (**borrowing more / purchasing ships / not controlling annual
   spending**).

3. <u>Interest expense</u> (**increased / decreased**) from 11/30/1999 to 11/30/2002, which MOST likely
   indicates that the company is (**borrowing more / purchasing ships / not controlling annual
   spending**).

4. Compute the <u>return on sales ratio</u> (Net income / Net sales) for the fiscal years ending on:

   11/30/02 _____%; 11/30/01 _____%   11/30/00 _____%   11/30/99 <u> 29.8 </u>%
   The strongest ratio was reported for the fiscal year ending in (**2002 / 2001 / 2000 / 1999**).

   Comment on the results.

5. Carnival Corporation appears to report a (**strengthening / steady / weakening**) operating position.
   Support your response with at least two observations.

6. In 2003, Carnival Corporation was the world's (**#1 / #2 / #3**) cruise line operating (**23 / 33 / 43**)
   ships, while it's primary competitor Royal Caribbean Cruises was operating 25 ships.

ANALYSIS of HASBRO, INC.

Purpose: · Understand and interpret amounts reported on the income statement.

HASBRO, INC.

Fiscal year ended ($ in millions)	12/29/02	12/30/01	12/31/00	12/26/99
Net sales	$ 2,816	$ 2,856	$ 3,787	$ 4,232
Cost of goods sold (COGS)	1,099	1,223	1,674	1,698
Gross profit	1,717	1,633	2,113	2,534
Selling, general, administrative expenses (SGA)	953	966	1,317	1,257
Research and development expenses (R&D)	154	126	635	712
Depreciation expense	95	122	158	173
Other operating expenses	296	208	107	64
Income from operations	219	211	(104)	328
Interest expense	77	104	115	69
Nonoperating income (loss)	(38)	(11)	(7)	15
Income from continuing operations before tax	104	96	(226)	274
Tax expense	29	35	(81)	85
Income from continuing operations	75	61	(145)	189
Nonrecurring items	(246)	(1)	-0-	-0-
Net income	$ (171)	$ 60	$ (145)	$ 189

Note: Subtotals and totals are shaded.

1. Since 12/26/1999, <u>net sales</u> have (**increased / decreased**) by $_____ million, which is a _____% change in sales. The greatest expense for Hasbro, Inc. is (**COGS / SGA / R&D / Depreciation**), while a close second is (**COGS / SGA / R&D / Depreciation**). Hasbro, Inc., the #2 toy maker, is a (**manufacturing / retail / service**) corporation. COGS is (**expected / not expected**) to be the largest expense for a manufacturing firm.

2. Since the fiscal year ended 12/26/1999, amounts spent on <u>research and development</u> have (**increased / decreased**). *Comment* on what this might indicate.

3. <u>Other operating expenses</u> (**increased / decreased**) from 12/26/1999 to 12/29/2002, which MOST likely indicates that the company is (**borrowing more / purchasing long-term assets / not controlling annual spending**).

4. Hasbro, Inc. received an income tax refund for the fiscal year ending in (**2001 / 2000 / 1999**). *Why?*

5. Compute income from continuing operations as a percentage of sales (Income from continuing operations / Net sales) for the fiscal years ending on:

    12/29/02 _____%;   12/30/01 _____%;   12/31/00 _____%;   12/26/99 _4.5 %_

    The strongest ratio was reported for the fiscal year ending in (**2002 / 2001 / 2000 / 1999**).

6. Hasbro appears to report a (**strengthening / steady / weakening**) operating position. *Support* your response with at least two observations.

TEST YOUR UNDERSTANDING
Analyzing the Income Statement

Purpose: · Understand and interpret amounts reported on the income statement.

Fiscal year ending ($ in millions)	CORP A 1/31/03	CORP B 12/31/02	CORP C 6/30/02	CORP D 12/31/02
Net sales	$244,524	$41,065	$28,365	$13,566
Cost of goods sold	191,838	24,419	5,191	8,131
Selling, general, and administrative expenses	39,967	9,916	6,957	2,455
Research and development expenditures	-0-	-0-	4,307	-0-
Other operating expenses	-0-	46,605	-0-	-0-
Interest expense	1,063	1,783	-0-	351
Nonoperating income (loss)	+870	(2,776)	(397)	+347
Income tax expense	4,487	140	3,684	1,042
Nonrecurring items	-0-	(54,122)	-0-	-0-
Net income	$ 8,039	$(98,696)	$ 7,829	$ 1,934
Outstanding shares (in millions)	# 4,430	# 4,455	# 5,406	# 866

1.   Using the amounts above, prepare a *multi-step income statement* for each corporation. Record the amounts in the form on the next page.

2.   For each corporation, prepare a *common-size statement* using the amounts from the classified balance sheet. Record your results in the shaded area provided on the next page.

3.   Use the descriptions below and the common-size income statements on the next page to identify each corporation. Circle the correct corporation.

ANHEUSER-BUSCH is the world's largest brewer and the largest beer producer in the United States with approximately half of the market share. It makes Budweiser, the nation's top-ranked beer, along with Bud Light, Michelob, and Busch. It is the largest recycler of aluminum cans in the world and one of the largest manufacturers of aluminum cans in the United States. It also operates amusement parks such as Busch Gardens and Sea World. Of the four corporations, its income from operations is 22% of sales. Anheuser Busch must be Corp .... **(A / B / C / D)**.
AOL TIME WARNER is a dominant presence in most forms of media including AOL Internet services, cable, entertainment, television networks, music, and publishing. In the 2001 merger, America Online contributed the world's #1 online service, CompuServe, Netscape, and several interactive services, while Time Warner contributed film and TV, music, cable networks and systems, publishing, and professional sports. For 2002, even though revenues increased 10% the company reported a huge net loss, resulting from a $54 billion nonrecurring item for the impairment of goodwill. AOL Time Warner must be Corp ....(A / B / C / D).
MICROSOFT is the world's #1 software company that develops, manufactures, licenses, and supports a variety of products and services, including its Windows operating systems and Office software suite. The company has expanded into markets such as video game consoles, interactive television, and Internet access. It is also targeting services for growth, looking to transform its software applications into Web-based services for enterprises and consumers. Microsoft has reached a tentative settlement to end an ongoing antitrust investigation, agreeing to uniformly license its operating systems and allow manufacturers to include competing software with Windows. Of the four corporations, Microsoft reports the greatest return-on-sales ratio. Microsoft must be Corp ....(A / B / C / D).

WAL-MART is the largest retailer in the world with about 4,600 stores. Its sales are greater than Sears, Target, and Kroger combined. Its stores include Wal-Mart discount stores, Wal-Mart Supercenters that are a combination discount and grocery store, and Sam's Club membership-only warehouse stores. Most Wal-Mart stores are in the United States, but international expansion has made it the #1 retailer in Canada and Mexico. Wal-Mart also has operations in South America, Asia, and Europe. Wal-Mart is rated #1 on the 2002 Fortune 500 list. Of the four corporations, Wal-Mart reports the lowest gross margin percentage. Wal-Mart must be Corp...(A / B / C / D).

MULTI-STEP INCOME STATEMENT
Common-Size Statements

($ in millions)	CORP A fye 1/31/03		CORP B fye 12/31/02		CORP C fye 6/30/02		CORP D fye 12/31/02	
Net sales	$	%	$	%	$	%	$	%
Cost of goods sold		%		%		%		%
Gross margin		%		%		%		%
Operating expenses		%		%		%		%
Income from operations		%		%		%		%
Other gains (losses)		%		%		%		%
Income before income tax		%		%		%		%
Income tax expense		%		%		%		%
Income from continuing operations		%		%		%		%
Nonrecurring items		%		%		%		%
Net income	$	%	$	%	$	%	$	%

* *Note*: Differences may occur due to rounding error.

4. Review the financial information above and *comment* on at least three items that you find of significance or of interest.

CHAPTER 4

ANALYZING THE STATEMENT OF CASH FLOWS

PURPOSE: Chapter 4 introduces strategies for analyzing the statement of cash flows and then applies those strategies. Students identify and analyze operating, investing, and financing activities.

QUESTION: The primary source of cash for an established company with a strong cash position should be operating, investing, or financing activities? Read this chapter to find the answer.

FEATURED CORPORATIONS

Amazon.com, Inc. (AMZN Nasdaq) is the world's largest bookstore offering millions of books, CDs, DVDs, videos, and other products at its Web site. After years of expansion, the company is now focusing on profits. Founder Jeff Bezos and his family own about one-third of the company. www.amazon.com

Ford Motor Company (F NYSE) began a manufacturing revolution in the 1900s with its mass production assembly lines. Now the company is the world's largest pickup truck maker and the #2 producer of vehicles behind General Motors. Vehicles are produced under the names of Ford, Jaguar, Lincoln, Mercury, Volvo, and Aston Martin. Ford has a controlling interest in Mazda and has purchased BMW's Land Rover SUV operations. It also owns the #1 auto finance company, Ford Motor Credit, and Hertz, the world's #1 car-rental firm. The Ford family owns about 40% of the company's voting stock. www.ford.com

Pfizer Inc. (PFE NYSE) is a large pharmaceutical company offering products that include erectile dysfunction therapy Viagra, cardiovascular drug Norvasc, antidepressant Zoloft, and cholesterol-lowering Lipitor. It also makes the brands Visine, BenGay, Listerine, Certs, Dentyne, Efferdent, Benadryl, and Sudafed. Subsidiaries in the Pfizer pharmaceutical group include Warner-Lambert, Parke-Davis, and Goedecke. www.pfizer.com

Procter & Gamble (PG NYSE) is the #1 maker of household products. Twelve of its brands are billion-dollar sellers including Tide, Bounty, Charmin, Crest, Downy/Lenor, Folgers, Iams, Pampers, Pantene, Pringles, Always/Whisper, and Ariel. It also produces the soap operas *Guiding Light* and *As the World Turns* and in 2001 purchased Clairol. www.pg.com

Royal Caribbean Cruises Ltd. (RCL NYSE) is the world's second-largest cruise line (behind Carnival) providing cruises to Alaska, the Caribbean, and Europe on 25 different cruise ships. The firm's two cruise brands, Celebrity Cruises and Royal Caribbean International, carry over two million passengers a year to about 200 destinations. www.rccl.com

UAL Corporation (UAL NYSE) operates United Airlines, the world's #2 air carrier (behind AMR's American Airlines). United Airlines flies 540 jets to more than 130 destinations in the United States and 27 other countries. At the beginning of 2003, UAL was still reorganizing under bankruptcy protection. The employees control 55% of the airline. www.united.com

----

Numerous sources including *Hoover's Company Capsules*, **Hoover's, Inc., 2003.**

OPERATING ACTIVITIES

Purpose: · Understand operating activities on the statement of cash flows.

The statement of cash flows reports cash inflows and outflows for operating activities, investing activities, and financing activities.

1. Operating activities include cash transactions that primarily affect
    (**current assets / long-term assets / current liabilities / long-term liabilities / stockholders' equity**).
    (Circle the *two best* answers)

2. Circle *operating* to identify the transactions/events below that are recorded in the operating section of the statement of cash flows.

    (**Operating / Not**)   a. Receive cash from customers paying on account.
    (**Operating / Not**)   b. Pay rent for the next accounting period.
    (**Operating / Not**)   c. Purchase factory equipment.
    (**Operating / Not**)   d. Receive the utility bill for this accounting period.
                                                The bill will be paid next week.
    (**Operating / Not**)   e. Pay wages payable.

3. On the statement of cash flows, a positive amount indicates a cash (**inflow / outflow**), while a negative amount indicates a cash (**inflow / outflow**). Note: On the statement of cash flows, cash outflows may be identified by enclosing the amount within parentheses or preceding the amount with a minus sign.

    For operating activities, a net cash (**inflow / outflow**) is preferred.

4. a. Net income reported on the income statement is primarily based on (**accrual / cash**) accounting, while cash from operating activities reported on the statement of cash flows is primarily based on (**accrual / cash**) accounting.

    b. Net income includes (**sales revenue earned / cash received from customers**), while cash from operating activities includes (**sales revenue earned / cash received from customers**).

    c. Net income includes (**salary expense incurred / salaries paid**), while cash from operating activities includes (**salary expense incurred / salaries paid**).

5. Decision makers compare "net income" to "net cash from operating activities." To make these two amounts more comparable, it is preferable to report the same accounts on both the income statement and the operating activity section of the statement of cash flows.

    Which of the following accounts are used to compute net income?
    (**Interest revenue / Interest expense / Dividend revenue / Dividends paid**)

    *   *Interest revenue* (**is / is not**) reported on the income statement, therefore, *interest payments received* are reported as a(n) (**operating / investing / financing**) activity on the statement of cash flows.
    *   *Interest expense* (**is / is not**) reported on the income statement, therefore, *interest payments* are reported as a(n) (**operating / investing / financing**) activity on the statement of cash flows.
    *   *Dividend revenue* (**is / is not**) reported on the income statement, therefore, *dividend payments received* are reported as a(n) (**operating / investing / financing**) activity on the statement of cash flows.
    *   *Dividends paid* (**are / are not**) reported on the income statement, therefore, *dividends paid* are reported as a(n) (**operating / investing / financing**) activity on the statement of cash flows.

6. The operating activity section of the statement of cash flows can be reported using the direct or the indirect method. The <u>direct method</u> reports sources of cash and disbursements of cash during the accounting period. The <u>indirect method</u> reports net income followed by amounts adjusting accrual-based "Net Income" to cash-based "Net Cash from Operating Activities."

CASH FLOWS FROM OPERATING ACTIVITIES

Fiscal year ended ($ in 000s)	12/31/20X7
Cash from customers	$ 1,700,000
Cash from interest and dividend income	2,900
Cash paid to suppliers for inventory	(1,100,000)
Cash paid to employees	(360,000)
Cash paid for various expenses	(120,000)
Cash paid for interest expense	(80,000)
Net cash from operating activities	$ 42,900

a. Cash flows from operating activities above are reported using the (**direct / indirect**) method. *Explain* how you can tell.

b. *List* three transactions that result in a <u>cash inflow</u> from operating activities when using the direct method.

c. *List* three transactions that result in a <u>cash outflow</u> from operating activities when using the direct method.

7.

CASH FLOWS FROM OPERATING ACTIVITIES

Fiscal year ended ($ in 000s)	12/31/20X7
Net income (loss)	$ (10,000)
Depreciation expense	60,000
(Increase) decrease in accounts receivable	1,200
(Increase) decrease in inventory	900
Increase (decrease) in accounts payable	(9,600)
Other adjustments, net	400
Net cash from operating activities	$ 42,900

a. Cash flows from operating activities immediately above are reported using the (**direct / indirect**) method. Accrual-based net income of $_____ thousand is followed by adjustments to arrive at $_____ thousand in net cash from operating activities.
b. The most significant adjustment is (**depreciation expense / decrease in accounts payable**).
c. Depreciation expense is (**added / subtracted**) to compute net income. It is an expense that is incurred, but not paid out in cash. Because it is not paid out in cash, it must be (**added back / subtracted**) when adjusting "accrual-based" net income to "cash-based" net cash from operating activities.
d. The 20X7 adjustment for accounts receivable was (**added / subtracted**) because during 20X7 the accounts receivable account (**increased / decreased**) resulting in (**more / less**) cash collections than sales revenue for the company.

8. When using the <u>indirect method</u> to adjust from net income to cash from operating activities, identify whether the following are added (**+**), subtracted (**-**), or are (**Not**) adjusted.

   (**+** / **-** / **Not**) a. Revenues earned and received in cash.
   (**+** / **-** / **Not**) b. Noncash revenues reported on the income statement.
   (**+** / **-** / **Not**) c. Expenses incurred and paid in cash.
   (**+** / **-** / **Not**) d. Noncash expenses reported on the income statement.
   (**+** / **-** / **Not**) e. Depreciation expense.

9. Is it possible to report a net loss on the income statement and still report a net cash inflow from operating activities? (**Yes** / **No**) *Explain* why.

10.
PROCTER & GAMBLE COMPANY
CASH FLOWS FROM OPERATING ACTIVITIES

Fiscal year ended ($ in millions)	06/30/02	06/30/01	06/30/00
Net income (loss)	$ 4,352	$ 2,922	$ 3,542
Depreciation expense	1,693	2,271	2,191
(Increase) decrease in accounts receivable	96	(122)	64
(Increase) decrease in inventory	159	(67)	(176)
Increase (decrease)in accounts payable	684	801	(883)
Other adjustments, net	758	(1)	(63)
Net cash inflows (outflows) from operating activities	$ 7,742	$ 5,804	$ 4,675

Review cash flows from operating activities for Procter & Gamble above.

a. The (**direct** / **indirect**) method is used to report cash flows from operating activities for Procter & Gamble.

b. For the year ended 6/30/2001, the adjustment for accounts receivable was (added / **subtracted**) because during the year the accounts receivable account (**increased** / **decreased**) resulting in (**more** / **less**) cash collections than sales revenue for the company.

   If the accounts receivable balance was $2,809 million on 6/30/2000, then the balance would be $_____ million on 6/30/2001.

c. Procter & Gamble reports a (**strong** / **weak**) cash position for operating activities. *Support* your response with at least one observation.

11. Procter & Gamble is the #1 maker of household products. *List* three familiar brand names manufactured by Proctor & Gamble. (*Hint*: Refer to the descriptions at the beginning of the chapter.)

INVESTING ACTIVITIES

Purpose: · Understand investing activities on the statement of cash flows.

1. Investing activities include cash transactions that primarily affect the purchasing and selling of (**current assets / long-term assets / current liabilities / long-term liabilities / stockholders' equity**).

(Circle the *one best* answer)

2. Circle *investing* to identify the transactions/events below that are recorded in the investing section of the statement of cash flows.

(**Investing / Not**)   a. Sell equipment at a loss.
(**Investing / Not**)   b. Pay rent for the next accounting period.
(**Investing / Not**)   c. Purchase factory equipment.
(**Investing / Not**)   d. Purchase 100 shares of Coca-Cola common stock.
                 The intent is to hold the security long term.
(**Investing / Not**)   e. Issue additional shares of your company's common stock.

3.   a. A net cash inflow from investing activities may indicate a company is (**purchasing / selling**) more property, plant, and equipment.

   b. If a company is selling income-producing assets, future revenues may be (**higher / lower**) as a result. Generally, this situation would be considered (**favorable / unfavorable**).

   c. However, if the asset being sold is an unprofitable division, then the situation would be considered (**favorable / unfavorable**).

   d. A net cash inflow from investing activities may also indicate a company is (**purchasing / selling**) investments.

   e. If the reason for selling the investments is to take profits, this would be considered (**favorable / unfavorable**).

   f. If the reason for selling the investments is to finance operations, this would be considered (**favorable / unfavorable**).

4. *List* three transactions that result in a <u>cash inflow</u> from investing activities.

5. *List* three transactions that result in a <u>cash outflow</u> from investing activities.

6. For investing activities, a net cash (**inflow / outflow**) is generally preferred.

7.

PROCTER & GAMBLE COMPANY
CASH FLOWS FROM INVESTING ACTIVITIES

Fiscal year ended ($ in millions)	06/30/02	06/30/01	06/30/00
(Increase) decrease in property, plant, and equipment	$ (1,452)	$ (1,698)	$ (2,599)
(Acquisition) disposition of subsidiaries, businesses	(5,471)	(138)	(2,967)
(Increase) decrease in security investments	88	(7)	221
Net cash inflows (outflows) from investing activities	$ (6,835)	$ (1,843)	$ (5,345)

Refer to the investing activity section of the statement of cash flows displayed above for Procter & Gamble to answer the following questions.

a. For (Increase) decrease in property, plant, and equipment Procter & Gamble had a net cash (**inflow / outflow**), which indicates the company is (**purchasing / selling**) more property, plant, and equipment. In general, this is an indication of a(n) (**expanding / contracting**) business.

   Because property, plant, and equipment are income-producing assets, additional purchases are expected to produce (**higher / lower**) future revenues.

   In general, the purchase of property, plant, and equipment is considered (**favorable / unfavorable**).

b. For (Acquisition) disposition of subsidiaries, businesses Procter & Gamble had a net cash (**inflow / outflow**), which indicates the company is (**acquiring / disposing of**) subsidiaries or businesses. In general, this is an indication of a company that is (**expanding / contracting**) and is considered (**favorable / unfavorable**).

c. In (**2002 / 2001 / 2000**), Procter & Gamble sold more security investments than it purchased. If Procter & Gamble sold the investments to realize a gain on appreciation, this would be considered (**favorable / unfavorable**).

d. Procter & Gamble reports a (**strong / weak**) cash position for investing activities. *Support* your response with at least two observations.

FINANCING ACTIVITIES

Purpose: · Understand financing activities on the statement of cash flows.

1.   Financing activities include cash transactions that primarily affect
(current assets / long-term assets / current liabilities / long-term liabilities / stockholders' equity).
(Circle the *two best* answers)

2.   Circle *financing* to identify the transactions/events below that are recorded in the financing
section of the statement of cash flows.

> **(Financing / Not)**   a. Purchase your company's common stock currently
> outstanding.
> **(Financing / Not)**   b. Declare and pay a cash dividend.
> **(Financing / Not)**   c. Receive dividend revenue.
> **(Financing / Not)**   d. Call a bond payable currently outstanding.
> **(Financing / Not)**   e. Pay wages payable.

3.   a. A net cash *inflow* from financing activities may indicate the company is **(issuing / repaying)** debt.

   b. If the debt is issued to finance growth and expansion, it is considered **(favorable / unfavorable)**.

   c. However, if the debt is issued because cash from operating activities is insufficient, it would be
   considered **(favorable / unfavorable)**.

   d. A net cash *inflow* from financing activities may indicate a company is **(issuing / repurchasing)**
   more of its own common stock.

   e. The ability to attract equity investors is considered **(favorable / unfavorable)**.

   f. A net cash **(inflow / outflow)** may indicate the company is paying cash dividends, which is
   generally considered **(favorable / unfavorable)**.

4.   *List* three transactions that result in a <u>cash inflow</u> from financing activities.

5.   *List* three transactions that result in a <u>cash outflow</u> from financing activities.

6.
PROCTER & GAMBLE COMPANY
CASH FLOWS FROM FINANCING ACTIVITIES

Fiscal year ended ($ in millions)	06/30/02	06/30/01	06/30/00
Dividends paid to shareholders	$ (2,095)	$ (1,943)	$ (1,796)
Increase (decrease) in debt	2,623	38	3,030
Increase (decrease) in equity	(331)	(1,109)	(1,430)
Net cash inflows (outflows) from financing activities	$ 197	$ (3,014)	$ (196)

Refer to the financing activity section of the statement of cash flows displayed above for Procter & Gamble to answer the following questions.

   a. Procter & Gamble is (**paying / not paying**) <u>dividends</u>.

   b. For <u>(Increase) decrease in debt</u> Procter & Gamble had a net cash (**inflow / outflow**), which indicates the company is (**issuing / repaying**) debt. In general, this indicates the company is relying (**more / less**) on debt financing.

   c. Debt financing (**increases / has no affect on / decreases**) shares outstanding, so earnings are (**shared / not shared**) with additional shareholders.

   d. For <u>(Increase) decrease in equity</u> Procter & Gamble had a net cash (**inflow / outflow**), which indicates the company is (**issuing / purchasing**) its own stock.

   e. A company's own stock that is bought back with the intent to reissue to shareholders in the future is referred to as (**common / preferred / treasury**) stock. Buying back a company's own stock (**increases / decreases**) shares outstanding, which results in (**greater / less**) earnings per share for shareholders. In general, shareholders regard this (**favorably / unfavorably**).

   f. Procter & Gamble's cash position for financing activities (**is / is not**) appealing to shareholders. *Support* your response with at least two observations.

OPERATING, INVESTING, OR FINANCING?

Purpose: · Identify operating, investing, and financing activities on the statement of cash flows.

1. The primary source of cash for an established company with a strong cash position should be (**operating / investing / financing**).

2. Identify the following transactions as **Operating**, **Investing**, or **Financing** by circling **O**, **I**, or **F**.

   (**O / I / F**)   a.   Cash received from customers.

   (**O / I / F**)   b.   Purchase of treasury stock.

   (**O / I / F**)   c.   Purchase of property, plant, and equipment.

   (**O / I / F**)   d.   Pay back long-term debt.

   (**O / I / F**)   e.   Pay interest expense.

   (**O / I / F**)   f.   Receive dividend revenue.

   (**O / I / F**)   g.   Declare and pay cash dividends to common shareholders.

3. If the following is a *cash* transaction identify it as **Operating**, **Investing**, or **Financing** by circling **O**, **I**, or **F**. If the following is a *noncash* transaction identify it by circling **N**.

   (**O / I / F / N**)   h.   Record depreciation expense.

   (**O / I / F / N**)   i.   Pay wages.

   (**O / I / F / N**)   j.   Record a 2-for-1 stock split.

   (**O / I / F / N**)   k.   Sell equipment for cash. Report a loss on the sale.

   (**O / I / F / N**)   l.   Accrue interest expense at year end.

4. For a note receivable, receiving repayment of principal is a(n) (**operating / investing / financing**) activity, while receiving an interest payment is a(n) (**operating / investing / financing**) activity.

5. For a loan payment, paying the principal is a(n) (**operating / investing / financing**) activity, while paying the interest is a(n) (**operating / investing / financing**) activity.

6. Issuing common stock to shareholders is a(n) (**operating / investing / financing**) activity, and paying cash dividends to those shareholders is a(n) (**operating / investing / financing**) activity.

Activity 40   **OPERATING, INVESTING, OR FINANCING?**

Purpose: · Identify operating, investing, and financing activities on the statement of cash flows.
                 · Understand the amount reported and whether the transaction results in an inflow or
                   an outflow of cash.

Kristin Incorporated is preparing a statement of cash flows using the *direct method*. For each transaction
*   Identify the following transactions as Operating, Investing, or Financing by circling **O, I,** or **F.**
*   Record the **$ amount** to be reported. Designate cash inflows as a positive amount and cash outflows
    as a negative amount within parentheses.

1.   Sell $2,000 of inventory to customers for $5,000 cash.   **(O / I / F)** $_____

2.   Sell equipment with a book value (carrying value)
      of $65,000 for $50,000 cash.   **(O / I / F)** $_____

3.   Borrow $100,000 from a bank at an annual interest rate of 7%.
      The note is due in three years.   **(O / I / F)** $_____

4.   Issue 1,000 shares of $100 par, 6%, preferred stock
      for $180 per share.   **(O / I / F)** $_____

5.   Pay $6,000 of accounts payable.   **(O / I / F)** $_____

6.   Sell an investment in the common stock of Microsoft for
      $12,000 in cash. The common stock was originally acquired
      for $5,000 and at the end of the previous accounting period
      the market value was $11,000.   **(O / I / F)** $_____

7.   On January 1st, purchase equipment for $50,000 cash down
      and a $150,000 long-term note payable.   **(O / I / F)** $_____

Activity 41   **LIST OPERATING, INVESTING, and FINANCING ACTIVITIES**

Purpose: · List typical operating, investing, and financing activities for both small and large companies.

1.   The statement of cash flows reports cash inflows and outflows for three basic activities. *Describe* typical operating, investing, and financing activities <u>for a locally operated hardware store with one owner</u>. Assume the owner leases space in a strip mall.

   a. Operating activities.

   b. Investing activities.

   c. Financing activities.

2.   *Comment* on how the typical operating, investing, and financing activities might differ between a major corporation such as <u>Wal-Mart or Sears</u> and the locally owned hardware store discussed above.

   a. Operating activities.

   b. Investing activities.

   c. Financing activities.

ANALYSIS of PFIZER INCORPORATED

Purpose: · Understand and interpret amounts reported on the statement of cash flows.

($ in millions)	2001	2000	1999
CASH FLOWS FROM OPERATING ACTIVITIES			
Net income (loss)	$ 7,752	$ 3,718	$ 4,972
Depreciation/amortization expense	1,068	968	905
(Increase) decrease in accounts receivable	(30)	(498)	(1,274)
(Increase) decrease in inventory	(102)	(436)	(278)
Increase (decrease) in accounts payable	(201)	807	378
Other adjustments, net	774	1,636	790
Net cash inflows (outflows) from operating activities	9,261	6,195	5,493
CASH FLOWS FROM INVESTING ACTIVITIES			
(Increase) decrease in property, plant, and equipment	(2,135)	(2,100)	(2,410)
(Increase) decrease in security investments	(5,043)	(1,882)	(1,524)
Other cash inflow (outflow)	(47)	229	28
Net cash inflows (outflows) from investing activities	(7,225)	(3,753)	(3,906)
CASH FLOWS FROM FINANCING ACTIVITIES			
Dividends paid to shareholders	(2,715)	(2,197)	(1,820)
Increase (decrease) in debt	3,511	(1,691)	2,099
Increase (decrease) in equity	(2,892)	183	(1,906)
Net cash inflows (outflows) from financing activities	(2,096)	(3,705)	(1,627)
Effect of exchange rate on cash	(5)	4	11
Net change in cash equivalents	(63)	(1,259)	(49)
Cash equivalents at year start	1,099	2,358	2,407
Cash equivalents at year end	$ 1,036	$ 1,099	$ 2,358

1. The primary source of cash is (**operating / investing / financing**) activities, which typically indicates a (**strong / weak**) cash position.

2. The company is (**purchasing / selling**) more property, plant, and equipment, which typically indicates a(n) (**expanding / contracting**) business.

3. During (**2001 / 2000 / 1999**), the company borrowed additional debt, which might indicate the assumption of (**more / less**) financial risk.

4. During (**2001 / 2000 / 1999**), the company purchased more of its own stock, which is generally considered (**favorable / unfavorable**).

5. The company is (**paying / not paying**) dividends.

6. Overall, Pfizer reports a (**strong / weak**) cash position.
   Support your response with at least two observations.

7. Pfizer's products include the much-acclaimed, prescription drug (**Ibuprofen / Tylenol / Viagra**) that treats impotence.

ANALYSIS of AMAZON.COM, INC.

Purpose: · Understand and interpret amounts reported on the statement of cash flows.

($ in thousands)	2002	2001	2000
CASH FLOWS FROM OPERATING ACTIVITIES			
Net income (loss)	$ (149,132)	$ (567,277)	$ (1,411,273)
Depreciation/amortization expense	87,752	265,742	406,232
(Increase) decrease in accounts receivable	(32,948)	20,732	(8,585)
(Increase) decrease in inventory	(51,303)	30,628	46,083
Increase (decrease) in accounts payable	156,542	(44,438)	22,357
Other adjustments, net	163,380	174,831	814,744
Net cash inflows (outflows) from operating activities	174,291	(119,782)	(130,442)
CASH FLOWS FROM INVESTING ACTIVITIES			
(Increase) decrease in property, plant, and equipment	(39,163)	(50,321)	(134,758)
(Increase) decrease in security investments	(82,521)	(196,775)	361,269
Other cash inflow (outflow)	-0-	(6,198)	(62,533)
Net cash inflows (outflows) from investing activities	(121,684)	(253,294)	163,978
CASH FLOWS FROM FINANCING ACTIVITIES			
Dividends paid to shareholders	-0-	-0-	-0-
Increase (decrease) in debt	(14,795)	(9,575)	648,450
Increase (decrease) in equity	121,689	116,456	44,697
Net cash inflows (outflows) from financing activities	106,894	106,881	693,147
Effect of exchange rate on cash	38,471	(15,958)	(37,557)
Net change in cash equivalents	197,972	(282,153)	689,126
Cash equivalents at year start	540,282	822,435	133,309
Cash equivalents at year end	$ 738,254	$ 540,282	$ 822,435

1. Review _operating activities_ and *comment* on what your observations indicate.

2. Review _investing activities_ and *comment* on what your observations indicate.

3. Review _financing activities_ and *comment* on what your observations indicate.

4. Amazon.com reports a (**strengthening / weakening**) cash position.
   Support your response with at least two observations.

5. Amazon.com is the world's (**largest / #2 / #3**) bookstore.

TEST YOUR UNDERSTANDING
Statement of Cash Flows

Purpose: · Understand and interpret amounts reported on the statement of cash flows.

COMPANY ($ in millions)	OPERATING	INVESTING	FINANCING
Ford 2001	$ 22,764	$ (17,169)	$ (2,976)
Royal Caribbean Cruises 2001	634	(1,784)	1,700
United Airlines (UAL) 2001	(160)	(1,969)	2,138

1. Answer the following questions by referring to the statement of cash flow information above.

   a. The company that appears to be borrowing money to finance operating activities is (**Ford / Royal Caribbean / United Airlines**).

   b. The company that appears to be borrowing money to expand and grow is (**Ford / Royal Caribbean / United Airlines**).

   c. The company that appears to be using amounts from operating activities to purchase property, plant, and equipment, repay debt, and pay dividends is (**Ford / Royal Caribbean / United Airlines**).

   d. The company that appears to have the *weakest* cash position is (**Ford / Royal Caribbean / United Airlines**). *Identify* at least two observations that support your response.

2. *Identify* what the statement of cash flows reveals about a company that the income statement does not.

3. *Explain* why "Net Cash from Operating Activities" includes interest revenue, interest expense, and dividend revenue, but not dividends paid.

CHAPTER 5

FURTHER RATIO ANALYSIS

PURPOSE: Chapter 5 reinforces the information provided by various financial ratios and introduces industry norms.

QUESTION: Industry average information is reported using which four-digit code? Read this chapter for the answer.

Note: Ratios are also covered in Activities 5-9.

FEATURED CORPORATIONS

Bristol-Myers Squibb Company (BMY NYSE) is a global producer and distributor of a variety of pharmaceuticals and related healthcare products. Most revenues come from prescription pharmaceuticals that treat cardiovascular disease, cancer, and infections. Major brands include Excedrin. www.bms.com

Coca-Cola Company, The (KO NYSE) was established in 1886 and is now the world's largest soft drink company operating in approximately 200 countries and commanding approximately 50% of the global soft-drink market. The firm, which does no bottling, sells about 300 drink brands, including Coca-Cola, Sprite, Barq's, Minute Maid, and Dasani and Evian water. www.cocacola.com

Deckers Outdoor Corporation (DECK Nasdaq) is in the shoe business and markets the Teva sports sandal, a cross between a hiking boot and a flip-flop used for walking, hiking, rafting, and other outdoor activities. While imitations flood the market, Teva is only offered in high-end outlets, which create a superior brand image for the sandals. The company's other product lines include Simple casual footwear and Ugg sheepskin boots and shoes. The founder and CEO of the company, Douglas Otto, owns about 35% of the company. www.deckers.com

Gap Inc., The (GPS NYSE) operates approximately 4,200 clothing stores including casual styles at The Gap, GapKids, and BabyGap, fast-growing budget Old Navy, and the chic Banana Republic. All Gap clothing is private-label merchandise made specifically for the company. From the design board to store displays, the company controls all aspects of its trademark casual look. The founding Fisher family owns about a third of the company. www.gap.com

General Motors Corporation (GM NYSE) is the world's #1 maker of cars and trucks, with brands such as Buick, Cadillac, Chevrolet, GMC, Pontiac, Saab, and Saturn. It also designs and manufactures locomotives (GM Locomotive) and heavy-duty transmissions (Allison Transmission). Other nonautomotive operations include DirecTV (Hughes Electronics) and subsidiary GMAC provides financing. www.gm.com

Home Depot Inc., The (HD NYSE) is the world's largest home improvement chain and second-largest retailer after Wal-Mart. It owns and operates 1,500 do-it-yourself warehouse retail stores in the United States, Canada, and Latin America. These stores offer building materials, home improvement products, and related furnishings. www.homedepot.com

IHOP Corporation (IHP NYSE) operates the International House of Pancakes restaurant chain with over 1,000 IHOP restaurants located in 41 states and Canada. Over 90% of the restaurants are franchised. www.ihop.com

Kroger Co., The (KR NYSE) is the #1 pure grocery chain in the United States, but Wal-Mart has overtaken Kroger as the largest seller of groceries. Kroger operates about 3,600 stores coast-to-coast under some two dozen names, including more than 2,400 supermarkets, 800 convenience stores under names such as Quik Stop and Kwik Shop, and 100 Fred Meyer supercenters offering groceries, general merchandise, and jewelry. www.kroger.com

May Department Stores Company, The (MAY NYSE) is the #2 upscale department store operator in the US, behind Federated Department Stores. May Department Stores operate about 445 department stores in 37 states under a dozen names including Lord & Taylor, Foley's, Filene's, and Hecht's. The company primarily sells to middle- and upper-middle income buyers, but is striving to reach younger customers with trendy brands and its matrimonial division. www.maycompany.com

Oracle Corporation (ORCL Nasdaq) is a leading provider of systems software, offering a variety of business applications that includes software for data warehousing, customer relationship management, and supply chain management. Oracle's software runs on a broad range of computers including mainframes, workstations, desktops, laptops, and handheld devices. Oracle also provides consulting, support, and training services. www.oracle.com

PepsiCo, Inc. (PEP NYSE) is the world's #2 soft-drink maker and the world's #1 maker of snacks. Beverages include Pepsi (the #2 soft drink), Mountain Dew, Slice, Tropicana Juices (the world's leading juice manufacturer), Aquafina bottled water, All-Sport, Dole juices, and Lipton tea. PepsiCo also owns Frito-Lay, the world's #1 maker of snacks such as corn chips (Doritos, Fritos) and potato chips (Lay's, Ruffles, WOW!). www.pepsico.com

Procter & Gamble (PG NYSE) is the #1 maker of household products. Twelve of its brands are billion-dollar sellers including Tide, Bounty, Charmin, Crest, Downy/Lenor, Folgers, Iams, Pampers, Pantene, Pringles, Always/Whisper, and Ariel. It also produces the soap operas *Guiding Light* and *As the World Turns* and in 2001 purchased Clairol. www.pg.com

----

Numerous sources including *Hoover's Company Capsules*, Hoover's, Inc., 2003.

RESEARCHING INDUSTRY NORMS

Purpose: · Introduce the concept of industry norms and how to research these averages.

Investors and creditors evaluate a corporation using many ratios that when reviewed together help to give an overall impression of corporate financial strength.

Meaning is added to a ratio by comparing that ratio to industry norms or averages since ratios indicating success may vary by industry. A good example of industry differences is illustrated by the inventory turnover ratio. The rate at which a grocery store is expected to sell items of inventory is much quicker than a department store. This makes sense since a grocery store carries perishable goods that spoil if not sold fairly quickly, while a department store carries nonperishables.

Meaning is also added to a ratio by comparing that ratio to ratios of previous years. Trends can then be evaluated as either favorable or unfavorable.

RESEARCHING INDUSTRY NORMS
Step one: Obtain the industry classification code for the company.
There are two widely used industry classification systems: the Standard Industrial Classification (SIC) system and the North American Industry Classification System (NAICS). NAICS was developed in 1997 to replace the SIC system; however, many financial institutions and governmental agencies, including the Securities and Exchange Commission (SEC), continue to use the SIC system. Therefore, this text will use the SIC system.

The Standard Industrial Classification code is a coding system used to report information on U.S. businesses. It divides corporations into 10 major groups that are further divided into major categories. The first two digits refer to the Major Group code and describe the general nature of the activity. The final two digits refer to the specific activity. For example, the primary SIC code for General Motors is 3711. The 37 refers to the major group code for transportation equipment, and the 11 specifically to motor vehicles and car bodies. Many corporations engage in more than one type of business. The primary SIC code refers to the type of business with the largest volume of sales. The secondary SIC codes are listed in descending order according to sales volume.

Step two: Research the industry average information using the SIC code or by the NAICS. References for industry average information include:
  Almanac of Business and Industrial Financial Ratios, by Leo Troy, published by Prentice Hall
  Industry Norms and Key Business Ratios, Dun and Bradstreet, Inc.
  Standard and Poor's Industry Surveys
  Mergent's Industry Review
  and various others including online resources and industry specific publications.

Refer to the above information to answer the following questions.
1.   To get an overall impression of corporate financial strength, investors and creditors should evaluate (**many ratios / only one or two ratios**).

2.   Industry norms for many ratios (**are the same / vary**) between industries.

3.   A trend analysis of a ratio (**adds meaning to / confuses**) the evaluation.

4.   Industry average information is reported by the four-digit _____
  _____ _____code.

5.   The primary SIC code refers to the portion of the business with the greatest (**sales revenue / assets / market valuation**).

ACID-TEST (QUICK) RATIO

Purpose: · Understand the information provided and the expected range of the Acid-Test Ratio.

The **acid-test ratio** compares assets that can be quickly liquidated to current liabilities. The acid-test ratio is a measure of the ability to pay current debts. It is a measure of short-term liquidity.

$$\text{ACID-TEST RATIO} = \frac{\text{Cash} + \text{Short-term investments} + \text{Net current receivables}}{\text{Current liabilities}}$$

Home Depot	**02/03/02**	**01/28/01**	**01/30/00**
	0.53	0.23	0.21
IHOP	**12/31/01**	**12/31/00**	**12/31/99**
	1.21	0.94	0.85
PepsiCo	**12/29/01**	**12/30/00**	**12/25/99**
	0.76	0.76	0.73
Procter & Gamble	**6/30/02**	**6/30/01**	**6/30/00**
	0.53	0.55	0.44

1. Examine the acid-test ratios presented above. The ratios are primarily in the range of (**less than .20 / .20 through 1.00 / more than 1.00**).

2. Acceptable acid-test ratios vary by industry. For each corporation above, circle the acid-test ratio indicating the greatest ability to pay current liabilities for the three years of information presented.

3. The acid-test ratio for IHOP is (**increasing / decreasing**). This is generally considered to be a(n) (**favorable / unfavorable**) trend.

4. The acid-test ratio is very similar to the (**current ratio / debt ratio**), but it excludes inventory and prepaid expenses from the numerator. Inventory and prepaid expenses are current assets but are not considered to be highly liquid. The (**acid-test / current**) ratio will always report a higher value.

5. For the most recent year of information, the corporations not able to pay off all current liabilities at this time with quick assets are (**Home Depot / IHOP / PepsiCo / P & G**).

6. If the acid-test ratio is less than one, does this indicate the corporation is in trouble and unable to pay current liabilities when due? (**Yes / No**) *Explain.*

7. The information for both the numerator and denominator of this ratio come from the (**balance sheet / income statement / statement of cash flows**).

8. In financial publications, the acid-test ratio may be referred to as the (**net profit margin / quick / interest coverage**) ratio.

DAYS' SALES IN RECEIVABLES

Purpose: · Understand the information provided and the expected range of the days' sales in receivables ratio.

The **days' sales in receivables** ratio indicates, on average, how many days it takes to collect accounts receivable. This ratio measures how quickly accounts receivable are collected. It is a measure of efficiency.

$$\text{ONE DAY'S SALES} = \frac{\text{Net sales}}{\text{365 days}}$$

$$\text{DAYS' SALES IN RECEIVABLES} = \frac{\text{Average net accounts receivable}}{\text{One day's sales}}$$

DAYS' SALES IN RECEIVABLES

Kroger	2/02/02	2/03/01	1/29/00
	4.95 days	5.12 days	4.72 days
Oracle	**5/31/02**	**5/31/01**	**5/31/00**
	87.89 days	90.38 days	99.54 days
PepsiCo	**12/29/01**	**12/30/00**	**12/25/99**
	29.03 days	30.50 days	24.79 days
Procter & Gamble	**6/30/02**	**6/30/01**	**6/30/00**
	28.03 days	27.26 days	26.59 days

1. Examine the days' sales in receivables ratios presented above. The ratios are primarily in the range of (**less than 20 days / 20 through 70 days / more than 70 days**).

2. For each corporation above, circle the days' sales in receivables ratio indicating the year receivables were collected the quickest on average.

3. For the days' sales in receivables ratio a(n) (**increasing / decreasing**) trend is considered favorable.

4. The two corporations most likely to have credit terms of net 30 are (**Kroger / Oracle / PepsiCo / P&G**).

5. Credit sales are when the corporation extends credit to customers. Cash sales include cash, checks, and credit cards such as VISA and MasterCard. VISA and MasterCard are not considered credit sales because the corporation is not assuming the risk of nonpayment. VISA and MasterCard are assuming that risk. The corporation primarily selling goods for cash to customers is (**Kroger / Oracle / PepsiCo / P&G**).

ACCOUNTS RECEIVABLE TURNOVER

Purpose: · Understand the information provided and the expected range of the
                       accounts receivable turnover ratio.

The **accounts receivable turnover ratio** indicates, on average, how many times accounts receivable are collected annually. It measures the ability to collect from credit customers. It offers the same information as the days' sales in receivable ratio, but presents it in a different manner. It is a measure of efficiency.

ACCOUNTS RECEIVABLE TURNOVER =	Net credit sales
	Average net accounts receivable

ACCOUNTS RECEIVABLE TURNOVER

Kroger	**2/02/02**	**2/03/01**	**1/29/00**
	73.78	71.32	77.31
Oracle	**5/31/02**	**5/31/01**	**5/31/00**
	4.15	4.04	3.67
PepsiCo	**12/29/01**	**12/30/00**	**12/25/99**
	12.57	11.97	14.73
Procter & Gamble	**6/30/02**	**6/30/01**	**6/30/00**
	13.02	13.39	13.73

1. Examine the accounts receivable turnover ratios presented above. The ratios are primarily in the range of (**less than 5 / 5 through 18 / more than 18**).

2. For each corporation above, circle the accounts receivable turnover ratio indicating the year receivables were collected the quickest.

3. For the accounts receivable turnover ratio a(n) (**increasing / decreasing**) trend is considered favorable because it indicates a company is efficiently managing its receivables.

4. The accounts receivable turnover ratio offers the same information as the days' sales in receivable ratio, but presents it in a different manner. If one ratio is known, the other ratio can be computed.

   For example, an accounts receivable turnover ratio of 6 also indicates receivables were collected on average in 60 days. (360 days / 6 = 60 days)

   Calculate the average collection time period for the following accounts receivable turnover ratios.

   a. Accounts receivable turnover of 12   = _____ days on average to collect

   b. Accounts receivable turnover of 18   = _____ days on average to collect

INVENTORY TURNOVER

Purpose: · Understand the information provided by the inventory turnover ratio.
             · Understand that the expected range varies by industry.

The **inventory turnover ratio** indicates the number of times a company sells its average inventory level during the year. It measures how efficiently a company uses its investment in inventory. It is a measure of efficiency.

$$\text{INVENTORY TURNOVER RATIO} = \frac{\text{Cost of goods sold}}{\text{Average inventory}}$$

INVENTORY TURNOVER RATIOS

Deckers Outdoor	**2001**	**2000**	**1999**
	2.98	3.61	3.16
General Motors	**2001**	**2000**	**1999**
	13.71	13.50	12.03
Home Depot	**fye 2/03/02**	**fye 1/28/01**	**fye 1/30/00**
	5.63	5.32	5.53
Kroger	**fye 2/02/02**	**fye 2/03/01**	**fye 1/29/00**
	8.83	8.95	11.61

1. Examine the inventory turnover ratios presented above. The ratios above are primarily in the range of (**less than 4 / 4 through 15 / more than 15**).

2. Acceptable inventory turnover ratios vary by industry. For each corporation above, circle the ratio indicating inventory sold the quickest for the three years of information presented.

3. The inventory turnover ratio for Kroger has (**increased/decreased**), which is a(n) (**favorable / unfavorable**) trend.

4. In general, an increasing trend indicates the company is using its inventory (**more / less**) efficiently and a (**greater / lower**) investment in inventory is needed.

5. For the most recent year of information, the highest inventory turnover ratio is _____ reported by (**Deckers / GM / Home Depot / Kroger**).

6. For the most recent year of information, the lowest inventory turnover ratio is _____ reported by (**Deckers / GM / Home Depot / Kroger**).

7. Does your response to #5 and #6 above indicate one company is performing better than another company? (**Yes / No**) *Explain* your response.

Activity 50   **TIMES-INTEREST-EARNED**

Purpose: · Understand the information provided and the expected range of the
                      times-interest-earned ratio.

The **times-interest-earned** ratio (also referred to as the interest coverage ratio) measures the number of
times operating income covers interest expense. This ratio measures the ability to pay interest expense.
It is a measure of long-term solvency.

$$\text{TIMES-INTEREST-EARNED} = \frac{\text{Income from operations}}{\text{Interest expense}}$$

TIMES-INTEREST-EARNED

General Motors	2001	2000	1999
	1.2	1.7	2.1
May Department Stores	fye 2/02/02	fye 2/03/01	fye 1/29/00
	4.2	4.9	6.1
Oracle	fye 5/31/02	fye 5/31/01	fye 5/31/00
	171.4	166.5	536.6
PepsiCo	fye 12/29/01	fye 12/30/00	fye 12/25/99
	19.4	15.5	11.1

1. Examine the times-interest-earned ratios presented above. The ratios are primarily in the range of
   (**less than 4 / 4 through 10 / more than 10**).

2. For each corporation above, circle the ratio indicating the greatest ability to pay interest expense for
   the three years of information presented.

3. The times-interest-earned ratio for PepsiCo is (**increasing/decreasing**), which is a(n) (**favorable /
   unfavorable**) trend indicating a (**stronger / weaker**) ability to meet interest payment obligations.

4. Oracle's extremely high times-interest-earned ratio may indicate Oracle has (**a great amount of /
   very little**) debt.

5. For the most recent year of information, (**GM / May / Oracle / PepsiCo**) has the greatest ability to
   pay interest expense, while (**GM / May / Oracle / PepsiCo**) has the weakest ability to pay interest
   expense.

6. In general, does your response to #5 above indicate one company is a greater credit risk than another
   company? (**Yes / No**) *Explain* your response.

7. In financial publications, the times-interest-earned ratio may be referred to as the (**net profit margin /
   quick / interest coverage**) ratio.

GROSS MARGIN PERCENTAGE

Purpose: · Understand the information provided by the gross margin percentage.
· Understand that the expected range varies by industry.

The **gross margin percentage** compares gross margin to net sales revenue. It expresses gross profit as a percentage of sales. This ratio is the first measure of profitability reported on the income statement.

$$\text{GROSS MARGIN PERCENTAGE} = \frac{\text{Gross margin}}{\text{Net sales revenue}}$$

GROSS MARGIN PERCENTAGES

Bristol-Myers Squibb	2001	2000	1999
	71.3%	73.9%	73.1%

General Motors	2001	2000	1999
	18.8%	21.1%	23.0%

Kroger	fye 2/02/02	fye 2/03/01	fye 1/29/00
	27.3%	26.9%	26.5%

May Department Stores	fye 2/02/02	fye 2/03/01	fye 1/29/00
	31.1%	31.6%	32.4%

1. For each corporation above, circle the strongest ratio for the three years of information presented.

2. In 2001, Bristol-Myers Squibb generated _____ cents of gross profit for each dollar of sales.

3. In 2001, it cost General Motors _____ cents of each sales dollar to manufacture cars and trucks, leaving _____ cents of each sales dollar to cover all remaining operating expenses, interest costs, income taxes, and profits.

4. The gross margin percentage for Kroger is (**increasing / decreasing**), indicating (**greater / less**) profitability.

5. For the companies above, the gross margin percentage has (**remained fairly stable / fluctuated greatly**).

6. For the most recent year of information, the highest gross margin percentage is _____%
reported by (**BMS / GM / Kroger / May**), while the lowest gross margin percentage is _____%
reported by (**BMS / GM / Kroger / May**).

7. Does your response to #6 above indicate one company is performing better than another company?
(**Yes / No**) Explain your response.

8. The gross margin percentage is the (**first / second / last**) indication of profitability on the income statement.

9. The information for both the numerator and denominator of this ratio come from the (**balance sheet / income statement / statement of cash flows**).

RETURN ON ASSETS (ROA)

Purpose: · Understand the information provided and the expected range of the rate of return on total assets ratio.

The **rate of return on total assets** measures how effectively assets are used to generate a return for shareholders and creditors. Net income is the return earned by shareholders. Interest is the return earned by creditors. It is a measure of profitability.

$$\text{RETURN ON ASSETS} = \frac{\text{Net income + Interest expense}}{\text{Average total assets}}$$

RETURN ON ASSETS

General Motors	**2001**	**2000**	**1999**
	0.002	0.015	0.022
Home Depot	**fye 2/03/02**	**fye 1/28/01**	**fye 1/30/00**
	0.128	0.121	0.136
IHOP	**2001**	**2000**	**1999**
	0.063	0.063	0.062
Oracle	**fye 5/31/02**	**fye 5/31/01**	**fye 5/31/00**
	0.205	0.232	0.482

1. For each corporation above, circle the strongest ratio for the three years of information presented.

2. Companies invest in assets to generate additional revenues and profits. In 2001, Home Depot earned _____ cent(s) in profit for each dollar invested in assets.

3. For Oracle, the return on assets ratio has (**increased / decreased**), which is a(n) (**favorable / unfavorable**) trend.

4. For the most recent year of information, (**GM / Home Depot / IHOP / Oracle**) most effectively used assets to generate income.

5. For the most recent year of information, (**GM / Home Depot / IHOP / Oracle**) least effectively used assets to generate income.

6. Does your response to #4 and #5 above indicate one company is using assets more effectively to generate profits? (**Yes / No**) *Explain* your response.

RETURN ON EQUITY (ROE)

Purpose: · Understand the information provided and the expected range of the rate of return on common stockholders' equity.

The **rate of return on common stockholders' equity** compares the net income earned with amounts invested by common shareholders. It is a measure of profitability.

$$\text{RETURN ON EQUITY} = \frac{\text{Net income - Preferred dividends}}{\text{Average common stockholders' equity}}$$

RETURN ON EQUITY

Home Depot	fye 2/03/02	fye 1/28/01	fye 1/30/00
	0.17	0.17	0.19
Oracle	fye 5/31/02	fye 5/31/01	fye 5/31/00
	0.36	0.40	0.97
PepsiCo	fye 12/29/01	fye 12/30/00	fye 12/25/99
	0.31	0.30	0.30
Procter & Gamble	fye 6/30/02	fye 6/30/01	fye 6/30/00
	0.36	0.28	0.34

1. For each corporation above, circle the strongest ratio for the three years of information presented.

2. During the fiscal year ended 2/03/02, Home Depot earned _____ cents in profits for each dollar invested by common shareholders.

3. The return on equity ratio for PepsiCo is (**increasing / decreasing**), which is a(n) (**favorable / unfavorable**) trend.

4. For the most recent year of information, (**Home Depot / Oracle / PepsiCo / P & G**) is using investments of common shareholder to generate the greatest amount of net income.

5. Does a greater return on equity ratio indicate that one company is able to generate more net income with amounts invested by common shareholders than another company? (**Yes / No**)

6. *Explain* why preferred dividends are subtracted to calculate return on equity.

7. When Return on Equity > Return on Assets it generally indicates the corporation
   a. is borrowing at a rate (**lower / higher**) than the rate earned by investors.
   b. is using financial leverage (**effectively / not effectively**).
   c. has a (**strong / weak**) financial position.

EARNINGS PER SHARE (EPS)

Purpose: · Understand the information provided by the earnings per share ratio.

The **earnings per share of common stock** indicate the amount of net income per one share of the company's common stock outstanding. It is a measure of profitability.

EARNINGS PER SHARE = $\dfrac{\text{Net income - Preferred dividends}}{\text{Number of shares of common stock outstanding}}$

EARNINGS PER SHARE

	2001	**2000**	**1999**
Deckers Outdoor	$0.18	$0.78	$0.33
General Motors	$1.79	$6.80	$8.70
IHOP	$1.98	$1.77	$1.61
Procter & Gamble	$3.26	$2.15	$2.61

1. Examine the earnings per share ratios presented above. The ratios are primarily in the range of **(less than $1 / $1 through $5 / more than $5)**.

2. For each corporation above, circle the strongest ratio for the three years of information presented.

3. The earnings per share of IHOP are **(increasing / decreasing)** which is a(n) **(favorable / unfavorable)** trend, indicating **(greater / less)** profitability per common share.

4. *Identify* at least two events that would result in greater earnings per share for a corporation.

5. The earnings per share ratio reflects **(only common / only preferred / both common and preferred)** earnings per share.

Note: The price/earnings (P/E) ratio compares the market value per share to earnings per share.
        The price/earnings (P/E) ratio = Market value per share / EPS

EARNINGS PER SHARE (EPS)

Purpose: · Understand that caution should be used when comparing earnings per share between companies.

For each situation below, additional information is presented regarding earnings per share (EPS). Comment on whether the information indicates Company A or Company B appears to be the better investment.

1.   <u>**Company A   EPS = $0.50**</u>   <u>**Company B   EPS = $2.00**</u>

<u>Net income</u> $1,000,000   <u>Net income</u> $1,000,000
# of shares   2,000,000   # of shares   500,000

Company (**A** / **B**) appears to be the better investment. *Explain* why.

2.   <u>**Company A   EPS = $ .50**</u>   <u>**Company B   EPS = $2.00**</u>

Current market price = $ 5/share   Current market price = $ 60/share

Company (**A** / **B**) appears to be the better investment. *Explain* why.

3.   <u>**Company A   19X1   19X2   19X3**</u>   <u>**Company B   19X1   19X2   19X3**</u>

EPS   0.10   0.20   0.50   EPS $8 $4 $2

Company (**A** / **B**) appears to be the better investment. *Explain* why.

4.   *Identify* two ways to enhance the meaning of a single earnings per share amount.

Activity 56   **PRICE/EARNINGS (P/E) RATIO**

Purpose: · Understand the information provided by the price/earnings ratio.

The **price/earnings ratio** indicates the market price of one dollar of earnings. It expresses the relationship between a company's earnings per share and the market price per common share. It is a measure of shareholder perception and evaluates a potential investment.

$$\text{PRICE/EARNINGS RATIO} = \frac{\text{Market price per share of common stock}}{\text{Earnings per share}}$$

PRICE/EARNINGS RATIOS on March 20, 2003

Bristol-Myers Squibb	15.50
Gap Inc.	27.70
General Motors	10.20
Home Depot	15.70
IHOP	12.60
May Department Stores	11.70
Oracle	29.00
PepsiCo	21.90
Procter & Gamble	25.30
DJIA companies average	23.00

1. Examine the price/earnings ratios presented above. The ratios are primarily in the range of (**less than 10 / 10 through 30 / more than 30**).

2. On March 20, 2003, one share of PepsiCo stock is selling for _____ times one year's earnings per share.

   On March 20, 2003, earnings per share for PepsiCo were $1.85 per share. Therefore, one share of PepsiCo stock was selling for approximately $ _____ per share.

3. In general, if investors have high future expectations for a company the P/E ratio will be (**higher / lower**).

4. Shareholders of Oracle have (**greater / lesser**) future expectations than the shareholders of IHOP.

5. A high PE ratio might indicate that a company's stock is (**overvalued / undervalued**), while a low PE ratio might indicate that a company's stock is (**overvalued / undervalued**).

6. A PE ratio that is much higher than the normal range might indicate that the market price or the earnings per share amounts are distorting the computation. The PE ratio of (**BMS / Gap / GM / Home Depot / IHOP / May / Oracle / PepsiCo / P & G / none of the companies**) appear(s) to be distorted.

DIVIDEND YIELD

Purpose: · Understand the information provided and the expected range of the dividend yield ratio.

The **dividend yield** indicates the portion of a stock's market value returned to the shareholder in the form of a dividend. It is a measure of dividends paid and helps evaluate a potential investment.

$$\text{DIVIDEND YIELD} = \frac{\text{Dividends per share of common stock}}{\text{Market price per share of common stock}}$$

DIVIDEND YIELD on March 20, 2003

Bristol-Myers Squibb	5.00%
Gap Inc.	0.60%
General Motors	5.90%
Home Depot	1.00%
IHOP	0.00%
May Department Stores	4.70%
Oracle	0.00%
PepsiCo	1.50%
Procter & Gamble	1.90%
DJIA companies average	2.12%

1. Examine the dividend yields presented above. The ratios are primarily in the range of
   (**less than 5% / more than 5%**).

2. As of March 20, 2003, General Motors issued dividends valued at _____ % of the market price of one share of stock.

   On March 20, 2003, the market price of one share of General Motor's common stock was approximately $34 per share. Therefore, dividends paid by General Motors were approximately $ _____ per share for the previous year.

3. (**BMS / Gap / GM / Home Depot / IHOP / May / Oracle / PepsiCo / P & G**) do not issue dividends. Not paying dividends (**is / is not**) a sign of financial weakness.

4. An investor wanting current dividend income would prefer a (**high / low**) dividend yield.

5. An investor wanting stock appreciation would prefer a (**high / low**) dividend yield.

6. Is a high dividend yield an indication of a superior company? (**Yes / No**) Why?

7. The dividend yield ratio (**can / cannot**) be compared between companies.

BOOK VALUE PER SHARE

Purpose: · Understand the information provided and the expected range of the book value per share
of common stock.
· Understand the difference between book value and market value per share.

The **book value per share of common stock** indicates the recorded accounting amount of common stockholders' equity per share of common stock outstanding. It helps evaluate a potential investment.

$$\text{BOOK VALUE PER SHARE} = \frac{\text{Total stockholders' equity - Preferred equity}}{\text{Number of shares of common stock outstanding}}$$

		MARKET VALUE per share	BOOK VALUE per share
Coca-Cola	3/20203	$ 41.56	$ 4.78
Deckers Outdoor Corporation	3/20203	3.96	7.13
General Motors	3/20/03	34.10	4.49
Home Depot	3/20203	24.63	7.71
IHOP	3/20203	23.95	15.08
Oracle	3/20/03	11.45	1.13
Procter & Gamble	3/20203	88.09	9.28

1. Examine the *book value per share* amounts presented above. The ratios are primarily in the range of (**less than $20 / more than $20**) per share.

   Book value is based primarily on (**historical cost / current value**).

2. Examine the *market value per share* information presented above. The ratios are primarily in the range of (**less than $20 / more than $20**) per share.

   Market value is primarily based on (**historical cost / current value**).

3. In general, (**market value / book value**) per share would be expected to be greater.
   Explain your response.

4. The above corporations with book value per share greater than market value per share include (**Coca-Cola / Deckers / GM / Home Depot / IHOP / Oracle / Procter & Gamble**). This is generally an indication of a (**wise / poor**) investment.

5. The Coca-Cola Company is over 100 years old. *Comment* on what may account for the large difference between the book value and the market value per share of Coca-Cola.

USING INDUSTRY NORMS

Purpose:
- Understand that reviewing many ratios helps give an overall impression of corporate financial strength.
- Understand that meaning is added to a ratio by comparing that ratio to industry norms or averages since success may vary by industry.

Industry Norm	RATIOS *November 2001*	THE GAP (GPS)	American Eagle Outfitters (AEOS)
1.7 0.4	**LIQUIDITY** Current ratio Acid-test (quick) ratio	1.2 0.3	2.4 0.7
52.1 Compute 3.7	**EFFICIENCY** Accounts receivable turnover Days' sales in receivables Inventory turnover	NC NC 4.1	59.0 Compute 6.3
38.2% 0.041 0.085 0.165% NA	**PROFITABILITY** Gross margin percentage Return on sales (Profit margin) Return on total assets (ROA) Return on common stockholders' equity (ROE) Earnings per share of common stock	39.0% 0.046 0.085 0.204 $0.75	37.1% 0.087 0.191 0.257 $1.52
0.19 12.9	**LONG-TERM SOLVENCY** Debt ratio Times-interest-earned ratio (Interest coverage ratio)	0.28 10.8	0.05 NC

18.9
NA
$5.42
	MARKET RATIOS
	Price-earnings ratio
	Dividend yield
	Book value per share of common stock
	Market stock quote:
	    Current
	    52-week low
	    52-week high
		20.10
		0.60%
		$3.77
		
		$15.08
		$11.12
		$34.98
			20.10
			0.00%
			$5.91
			
			$30.55
			$16.95
			$43.00

1. Evaluating a corporation by reviewing many ratios helps give an overall impression of corporate financial strength. Compare GAP Inc. and American Eagle Outfitters by *circling* the stronger ratio. Which company appears to be the stronger company? (**GAP Inc. / American Eagle**) Why?

2. Meaning is added to a ratio by comparing that ratio to industry norms since success may vary by industry. Compare American Eagle to the industry norms by placing *a box* around the stronger ratio. What do your observations indicate?

TEST YOUR UNDERSTANDING
A Review of Further Ratio Analysis

A listing of ratios covered in previous activities:

(**L E S P I**) Acid-test ratio   (**L E S P I**) Gross margin percentage

(**L E S P I**) Current ratio   (**L E S P I**) Return on sales (ROS)

(**L E S P I**) Days' sales in receivables   (**L E S P I**) Return on assets (ROA)

(**L E S P I**) Accounts receivable turnover   (**L E S P I**) Return on equity (ROE)

(**L E S P I**) Inventory turnover   (**L E S P I**) Earnings per share (EPS)

(**L E S P I**) Debt ratio   (**L E S P I**) Price/earnings ratio (PE)

(**L E S P I**) Times-interest-earned   (**L E S P I**) Dividend yield

                                 (**L E S P I**) Book value per share

1. Identify each of the ratios listed above by circling

   L if the ratio measures short-term *liquidity*.

   E if the ratio measures management *efficiency*.

   S if the ratio measures long-term *solvency*.

   P if the ratio measures *profitability*.

   I if the ratio is an evaluation tool for a potential stock *investment*.

2. Select from the above list one ratio of most concern to

   a. a supplier extending credit to a corporation for 60 days.

   b. a bank considering lending a large sum of money for 10 years.

   c. an investor primarily concerned with long-term growth.

3. Review the ratios below and circle your general impression of this company's *long-term solvency*: (**Adequate / Not adequate**). *Comment* on the information provided by each ratio and whether that information supports your response.

	Industry Average	20X5
Return on assets	0.10	0.06
Return on equity	0.18	0.04
Debt ratio	0.60	0.90
Times-interest-earned	2.50	0.80

4. Review the ratios below and circle your general impression of this company's *short-term liquidity*: (**Adequate / Not adequate**). *Comment* on the information provided by each ratio and whether that information supports your response.

	Industry Average	20X5
Current ratio	1.50	2.00
Acid-test ratio	0.80	1.10
Days' sales in receivables	35	30
Inventory turnover	6	8

CHAPTER 6

INTERPRETING and UNDERSTANDING
SPECIFIC ACCOUNTS

PURPOSE: Chapter 6 reinforces understanding of amounts reported on the financial statements. It also includes activities that examine the stock and bond market and benchmark current interest rates and the Dow Jones Industrial Average. Research activities require use of *The Wall Street Journal*, the Internet, and other business publications.

QUESTION: For property, plant, and equipment (PPE), is acquisition cost or book value added to calculate total assets? Read this chapter to find the answer.

FEATURED CORPORATIONS

Allied Waste Industries, Inc. (AW NYSE) is the #2 waste- hauler (Waste Management, Inc., is #1) that does business in every major facet of the nonhazardous solid waste industry. It serves 10 million customers through its network of collection companies, transfer stations, active landfills, and recycling facilities. The company has reorganized and is expanding through internal growth and vertical integration. www.alliedwaste.com

AOL Time Warner, Inc. (AOL NYSE) is a dominant presence in most forms of media including AOL Internet services, cable, entertainment, television networks, music, and publishing. In the 2001 merger, America Online brought the world's Number 1 online service, CompuServe, Netscape, and several interactive services, while Time Warner contributed film and TV, music, cable networks and systems, publishing, and professional sports. For 2002, even though revenues increased 10% to $41 billion the company reported a huge net loss, resulting from a $54 billion nonrecurring item for the impairment of goodwill. www.aoltimewarner.com

Berkshire Hathaway Inc. (BRK NYSE) is where billionaire Warren Buffett, one of the world's richest men, pools his investments. It operates in the insurance industry and uses the "float," the cash collected before insurance claims are paid out, to invest in a portfolio of businesses. Buffett and his wife Susan own about 40% of the company. www.berkshirehathaway.com

Coca-Cola Company, The (KO NYSE) was established in 1886 and is now the world's largest soft drink company operating in approximately 200 countries and commanding approximately 50% of the global soft-drink market. The firm, which does no bottling, sells about 300 drink brands, including Coca-Cola, Sprite, Barq's, Minute Maid, and Dasani and Evian water. www.cocacola.com

Disney Company, The Walt (DIS NYSE) is the #2 media conglomerate in the world behind AOL Time Warner, operating in four segments: media networks, studio entertainment, parks and resorts, and consumer products. Disney owns the ABC television network, 10 broadcast TV stations, and more than 60 radio stations. It also has stakes in several cable channels such as ESPN (80%) and A&E Television Networks (38%). Walt Disney Studios produces films through Touchstone, Hollywood Pictures, and Miramax. Walt Disney Parks and Resorts (Walt Disney World and Disneyland) are the most popular resorts in North America. disney.go.com

General Electric Company (GE NYSE) is one of the top players in a vast array of markets including: aircraft engines, locomotives and other transportation equipment, appliances (kitchen and laundry equipment), lighting, electric distribution and control equipment, generators and turbines, nuclear reactors, medical imaging equipment, and plastics. Its financial arm accounts for nearly half of the company's sales, making GE one of the largest financial services companies in the U.S. Other operations include the NBC television network. www.GE.com

International Business Machines Corporation (IBM NYSE) is the largest provider of computer hardware in the world. It is among the leaders in almost every market in which it competes, including mainframe and servers, storage systems, desktop and notebook PCs, and peripherals. The company's service arm is the largest in the world. IBM is also one of the largest providers of both software (behind Microsoft) and semiconductors. www.ibm.com

Oracle Corporation (ORCL Nasdaq) is a leading provider of systems software, offering a variety of business applications that includes software for data warehousing, customer relationship management, and supply chain management. Oracle's software runs on a broad range of computers including mainframes, workstations, desktops, laptops, and handheld devices. Oracle also provides consulting, support, and training services. www.oracle.com

Trump Organization, The is privately owned by Donald Trump and controls several New York real estate pieces including Trump International Hotel, Trump Tower (26 floors), 40 Wall Street, and 50% of the General Motors Building. Trump also has a 42% stake in Trump Hotels & Casino Resorts, which operate three casinos in Atlantic City, and 50% of the Miss USA, Miss Teen USA, and Miss Universe beauty pageants. (212) 832-2000

Numerous sources including *Hoover's Company Capsules*, Hoover's, Inc., 2003.

CASH AND CASH EQUIVALENTS

Purpose: · Reinforce understanding of cash and cash equivalents.

ORACLE CORPORATION

($ in millions)	05/31/02	05/31/01	05/31/00
Cash and cash equivalents	$ 3,095	$ 4,449	$ 7,429
Short-term investments	2,746	1,439	333
Receivables	2,329	2,714	2,790
Prepaid expenses	558	362	331
Property, plant, equipment, net	987	975	935
Other long-term assets	1,085	1,091	1,259
TOTAL Assets	$10,800	$11,030	$13,077

NOTES TO CONSOLIDATED FINANCIAL STATEMENTS

Cash, Cash Equivalents and Investments in Debt and Equity Securities.
Our investment portfolio consists of cash, cash equivalents, and investments in debt and equity securities. Cash and cash equivalents consist primarily of highly liquid investments in time deposits of major banks, commercial paper, United States government agency discount notes, money market mutual funds, and other money market securities with original maturities of 90 days or less. Short-term investments primarily consist of commercial paper, corporate notes, and Unites States government agency notes with original maturities of greater than 91 days but less than one year.

Source: Oracle Corporation. *Annual Report 5/31/2002.* Notes to the financial statements.

Refer to the information presented above to answer the following questions:

1. For Oracle, highly liquid investments with maturities of 90 days or less are classified as (**cash and cash equivalents / short-term investments / long-term investments**) and investments with maturities of greater than 91 days but less than one year are classified as (**cash and cash equivalents / short-term investments / long-term investments**).

2. The definition of cash equivalents is reported (**on the balance sheet / on the income statement / in the notes to the financial statements**).

3. For Oracle, cash and cash equivalents plus short-term investments total $_____ million on 5/31/02 that is _____% of total assets, which is (**more / less**) than the average company.

4. One measure of cash flow adequacy is (**free cash flow / the debt ratio / return on sales**), which is the amount of cash available from operations after paying for planned investments in property, plant, and equipment and other long-term assets.

5. Can a company ever have too much cash? (**Yes / No**)   Too little cash? (**Yes / No**)   Explain.

SHORT-TERM INVESTMENTS

Purpose: · Reinforce understanding of amounts reported on the financial statements for short-term investments.

12/31/20X1 BALANCE SHEET ACCOUNTS
Cash ....$ 30,000
Short-term investments -- Trading securities 200,000
Interest receivable... 1,000
Total current assets $231,000

20X1 INCOME STATEMENT ACCOUNTS
Unrealized loss on trading securities......................................$ 12,000
Interest revenue...4,000
Dividend revenue 5,000

Assume this is the *first year* of operation. Refer to the information presented above to answer the following questions:

1. Investments classified as short term are intended to be sold or liquidated in (**one year or less / more than one year**).

2. Trading securities are reported on the balance sheet at their (**acquisition cost / amortized cost / fair market value**). $_____ is the fair market value of the trading securities reported above. Since purchasing these trading securities, their market value has (**increased / decreased / can't tell**) by $_____. Since this is the first year of operation, these securities must have been originally purchased for $_____.

3. If these securities were sold next year, a(n) (**realized / unrealized**) loss would be reported if the selling price was less than the (**acquisition cost / fair market value at the end of last year / current fair market value**).

4. The amount of interest *earned* during this accounting period was $_____. Of this amount, $_____ was collected in cash during this accounting period and $_____ is the amount of cash to be received in the future.

5. The *other*, in *other* gains and losses (also referred to as *other* revenues and expenses), refers to *other* than (**operating / investing / financing**).

6. The income statement accounts listed above would be reported on a multi-step income statement as (**operating expenses / other gains and losses**).

7. As a result of the financial statement information listed above, 20X1 net income will (**increase / decrease**) by $ _____.

Activity 63   **ACCOUNTS RECEIVABLE**

Purpose: ·   Reinforce understanding of amounts reported on the financial statements for accounts receivable.

12/31/20X5 BALANCE SHEET ACCOUNTS

Accounts receivable .... $ 90,000
Allowance for uncollectible accounts...........................(4,000)
Accounts receivable, net 86,000

20X5 INCOME STATEMENT ACCOUNTS

Net sales revenue $800,000
Uncollectible account expense......................................15,000

Refer to the information presented above to answer the following questions:

1. The _allowance_ for uncollectible accounts is the portion of (**accounts receivable / net sales revenue**) that is estimated as uncollectible and is reported on the balance sheet as a (**current asset / long-term asset / current liability / long-term liability / stockholders' equity**).

2. The total amount customers owe the company on account on 12/31/20X5 is $_____. Of this amount, $_____ is estimated to be uncollectible and $_____ is estimated to be collectible. As a result of the financial statement information listed above, total assets will increase by $_____.

3. Uncollectible-account _expense_ is the portion of (**accounts receivable / net sales revenue**) that is estimated as uncollectible and reported as (**an operating expense / other gains and losses**) on a multi-step income statement. Above, sales revenue earned during 20X5 totals $_____ and of that amount $_____ is estimated to be uncollectible.

4. Uncollectible-account expense is a(n) (**estimated / known**) amount calculated (**at the end of / during**) each accounting period and recorded as an adjustment. This is an application of the (**cost / matching / reliability**) principle. The adjustment to record uncollectible-account expense changes (**total assets / net income / both / neither**). _Explain_ why.

5. Above, the (**allowance / direct write-off**) method is used to report uncollectible accounts. Using the above amounts, assume that $2,000 owed by Customer ABC was written off as uncollectible. After the write-off the accounts would report: Accounts receivable (**$88,000 / $90,000 / $92,000**), Allowance for uncollectible accounts (**$2,000 / $4,000 / $6,000**), and Accounts receivable, net (**$84,000 / $86,000 / $88,000**). The write-off of an uncollectible account changes (**total assets / net income / both / neither**). _Explain_ why.

Note: Accounts receivable, net is also referred to as net realizable value.
     Uncollectible-account expense is also referred to as doubtful-account expense or bad-debt expense.
     Other gain and losses is also referred to as other revenues and expenses.

Activity 64   **ETHICS AFFECTING FINANCIAL STATEMENT AMOUNTS**
                           Accounts Receivable

Purpose: · Understand the effect ethical decisions have on amounts reported on the financial
                     statements.

A manager of a small electronics store would like to expand and also sell computers. The expansion
would require seeking a loan from a local bank. The manager knows net income for this year is lower
than what is needed to qualify for additional financing at his current bank. The manager also realizes
some of the estimates used to calculate net income could be adjusted to make net income come within the
qualifying range for an additional loan.

1.   On the income statement, over-estimating uncollectible-account expense will result in

      (**understating / having no affect on / overstating**) operating expenses.

      (**understating / having no affect on / overstating**) net income.

2.   On the balance sheet, over-estimating uncollectible-account expense will result in

      (**understating / having no affect on / overstating**) the allowance for uncollectibles.

      (**understating / having no affect on / overstating**) accounts receivable, net.

3.   To qualify for the bank loan, the manager should (**over / under**) estimate uncollectible-account
      expense. *Explain* why.

4.   Is intentionally misstating an estimate ethical? (**Yes / No / Maybe**) *Explain.*

5.   Is intentionally misstating an estimate legal? (**Yes / No / Maybe**) *Explain.*

6.   List some possible consequences if bank officials detect the misstatement of the estimate.

7.   Discuss some ways the misstatement of uncollectible account expense could be detected by bank
      officials.

8.   In general, unethical decisions make the (**short term / long term**) appear better, but may result in
      huge (**short-term / long-term**) costs.

INVENTORY

Purpose: · Reinforce understanding of amounts reported on the financial statements for inventory as a result of using the LIFO cost-flow assumption.

GENERAL ELECTRIC COMPANY

Note 1: Summary of Significant Accounting Policies

Inventories. All inventories are stated at the lower of cost or realizable values. Cost for substantially all of GE's U.S. inventories is determined on a last-in, first-out (LIFO) basis. Cost of other GE inventories is primarily determined on a first-in, first-out (FIFO) basis.

Note 11: GE Inventories (Adapted)

December 31 ($ in millions)	2002	2001
Raw material and work in process	$ 4,894	$ 4,708
Finished goods	4,379	3,951
Unbilled shipments	372	312
	9,645	8,971
Less revaluation to LIFO	(606)	(676)
	$9,039	$8,295

Refer to Note 1 above to answer questions 1 and 2.

1. General Electric uses the (**FIFO / Weighted Average / LIFO**) inventory cost-flow assumption(s). *Hint*: Circle all that apply.

2. Does the answer for #1 comply with the Consistency Principle? (**Yes / No**) *Explain*.

Refer to Note 11 above to answer questions 3 through 7.

3. On December 31, 2002, the balance sheet would have reported inventories of (**$9,645 / $9,039**) million if the first-in, first-out (FIFO) method had been used to value all inventories and (**$9,645 / $9,039**) million if the last-in, first-out (LIFO) method were used to value the domestic portion of inventories.

4. Circle the effect the LIFO cost-flow assumption has had on reported financial statement amounts since GE began operations. As a result of using LIFO, GE has reported:
    a. $606 million (**more / less**) in ending inventory.
    b. $606 million (**more / less**) in cost of goods sold (COGS).
    c. $606 million (**more / less**) in income from continuing operations before tax.
    d. assuming a 40% tax rate, $242 million ($606 million x 40%) (**more / less**) in tax expense.

5. The revaluation to LIFO (**decreased / increased**) from 2001 to 2002, which indicates there probably (**was / was not**) a LIFO liquidation.

6. In a period of inflation, the cost-flow assumption resulting in the lowest taxable income is (**FIFO / Weighted Average / LIFO**). This tax benefit is achieved by allocating the higher, more current inventory costs to (**COGS / Ending Inventory**).

7. General Electric would appear more profitable if it used (**FIFO / LIFO**) to determine the value of all inventories. Would it really be more profitable? (**Yes / No**) *Explain*.

Activity 66   **ETHICS AFFECTING FINANCIAL STATEMENT AMOUNTS**
Inventory

Purpose: · Understand the effect ethical decisions have on amounts reported on the financial statements.

A manager of a men's clothing store receives a bonus based on the amount of gross margin earned by the department. This year the manager is only two thousand dollars short from qualifying for a sizable year-end bonus. The manager is in a position to have a portion of the inventory counted twice in the year-end physical inventory count. Cost of goods sold is adjusted for any changes to year-end inventory.

1.   On the balance sheet, double counting a portion of ending inventory will result in

       (**understating / having no affect on / overstating**) ending inventory.

       (**understating / having no affect on / overstating**) total assets.

2.   On the income statement, double counting a portion of ending inventory will result in

       (**understating / having no affect on / overstating**) cost of goods sold (COGS).

       (**understating / having no affect on / overstating**) gross margin.

3.   To qualify for the year-end bonus, the manager (**should / should not**) double count over two thousand dollars of ending inventory. *Explain* why.

4.   Is intentionally double counting ending inventory ethical? (**Yes / No / Maybe**) *Explain*.

5.   Is intentionally double counting ending inventory legal? (**Yes / No / Maybe**) *Explain*.

6.   List some possible consequences if upper management detects double counting of ending inventory.

7.   Discuss some ways the double counting of inventory could be detected by management.

PROPERTY, PLANT, AND EQUIPMENT

Purpose: · Reinforce understanding of property, plant, and equipment amounts reported on the financial statements.

12/31/20X5 BALANCE SHEET ACCOUNTS

Equipment $400,000
Accumulated depreciation .... (150,000)
Book value 250,000

20X5 INCOME STATEMENT ACCOUNTS

Depreciation expense $50,000
Gain on sale of equipment...7,000
Loss on sale of land..3,000

Refer to the financial statement information presented above to answer the following questions:

1. The amount originally paid (acquisition cost) to purchase the equipment was
    $_____, which was capitalized and recorded as a(n) (**long-term asset / expense**).

2. The portion of the equipment's original cost expensed since it was purchased is
    $_____. The cost allocated to 20X5 for use of the equipment is
    $_____. Assuming straight-line depreciation is used, it appears the equipment was
    purchased _____ years ago.

3. Depreciation expense is a(n) (**estimated / known**) amount recorded (**at the end of / during**) each
    accounting period as an adjustment, which is an application of the (**cost / matching / consistency**)
    principle. On a multi-step income statement, depreciation expense is reported as an (**operating
    expense / other gains and losses**).

4. The (**straight-line / double-declining-balance / neither**) method(s) of depreciation will result in
    greater depreciation the *first* year of an asset's useful life and the (**straight-line / double-declining-
    balance / neither**) method(s) will result in greater *total* depreciation over the asset's useful life.

5. Book value (**is / is not**) the same as current value. The primary purpose of depreciation is (**cost
    allocation / current valuation**). *Explain* what this means.

6. During the year, equipment was sold for $_____ more than (**acquisition cost /
    book value**) while land was sold for $_____ less than (**acquisition cost / book
    value**). The company got a better deal on the sale of the (**equipment / land / can't tell**). *Explain*.

7. As a result of the financial statement information above, total assets will (**increase / decrease**) by
    $_____ and 20X5 net income will (**increase / decrease**) by
    $_____.

8. By purchasing additional property, plant, and equipment, the company is investing in (**short-term /
    long-term**) income-producing assets that are expected to (**increase / decrease**) future revenues.

Activity 68   **ETHICS AFFECTING FINANCIAL STATEMENT AMOUNTS**
Property, Plant, and Equipment

Purpose: · Understand the effect ethical decisions have on amounts reported on the financial statements.

Financial analysts have predicted that net income will increase by 5% for a major corporation. Corporate management has suggested that the controller do what is necessary to meet these predictions. The controller decides to examine depreciation expense since the amount is based on estimates of useful life and residual value and GAAP allows choices with regard to depreciation methods.

1.   GAAP allows choices with regard to depreciation methods. In the first year of an asset's useful life, if the straight-line rather than the double-declining-balance depreciation method was used then:
     a.   reported depreciation expense will be (**lower / higher**), which leads to (**lower / higher**) net income.
     b.   reported accumulated depreciation will be (**lower / higher**), which leads to (**lower / higher**) book value and (**lower / higher**) total assets.

2.   To make net income appear as favorable as possible, the controller should choose the (**straight-line / double-declining-balance**) depreciation method for assets placed in service during the current year.

3.   Is intentionally choosing a depreciation method that reports higher net income ethical? (**Yes / No / Maybe**) Legal? (**Yes / No / Maybe**) *Explain*.

4.   Depreciation expense is based on estimates of useful life and residual value.
     a.   To make net income appear as favorable as possible, the controller should choose to (**shorten / extend**) an asset's useful life.
     b.   To make net income appear as favorable as possible, the controller should determine a (**lower / higher**) residual value for the asset.

5.   Is intentionally choosing an estimated useful life and residual value that report higher net income ethical? (**Yes / No / Maybe**) Legal? (**Yes / No / Maybe**) *Explain*.

6.   a.   For financial statement purposes, a company generally prefers to report (**lower / higher**) net income, and therefore, would choose the (**straight-line / double-declining-balance**) depreciation method.
     b.   For income tax purposes, a company generally prefers to report (**lower / higher**) taxable income, and therefore, would choose the (**straight-line / double-declining-balance**) depreciation method.
     c.   Is intentionally choosing one depreciation method for financial statement purposes and a different method for income tax purposes ethical? (**Yes / No / Maybe**) Legal? (**Yes / No / Maybe**)

7.   Identify at least three items that the controller can use to make net income appear more favorable with regard to the depreciation of assets placed in service during the current year that are both ethical and legal.

LONG-TERM INVESTMENTS

Purpose: · Reinforce understanding of amounts reported on the financial statements for long-term investments classified as available-for-sale securities.

1. Assume Winfield Corporation purchased 100 shares of Coca-Cola stock and 100 shares of IBM stock on 1/2/20X1. These equity securities are classified as available-for-sale because the intent is to hold them for several years. Refer to the related financial information below to answer the following questions.

	Fair Market Value			Cost
	12/31/20X3	**12/31/20X2**	**12/31/20X1**	**1/2/20X1**
COCA-COLA (100 shares)	$ 7,400	$ 5,300	$ 4,500	$ 4,600
IBM (100 shares)	11,400	7,600	6,000	10,000
Total	$18,800	$12,900	$10,500	$14,600

2. Complete the chart below to reflect how the above information would be reported on the financial statements.

BALANCE SHEET	12/31/20X3	12/31/20X2	12/31/20X1
ASSETS: Long-term investments	$	$	$
SE: Accumulated other comprehensive income -- *Unrealized gain/(loss) on investments*	$	$	$
INCOME STATEMENT	**20X3**	**20X2**	**20X1**
Other comprehensive income -- *Unrealized gain/(loss) on investments*	$	$	$
STATEMENT OF CASH FLOWS	**20X3**	**20X2**	**20X1**
INVESTING ACTIVITIES: Cash inflows (outflows)	$	$	$

3. When available-for-sale securities increase in value, this event will:
   a. (**increase / decrease / have no effect on**) total assets,
   b. (**increase / decrease / have no effect on**) net income,
   c. (**increase / decrease / have no effect on**) comprehensive income, and
   d. (**increase / decrease / have no effect on**) stockholders' equity.

4. Assume the 100 shares of Coca-Cola stock were sold for $76 per share during 20X4. As a result, the 20X4 income statement would report a (**realized / unrealized**) gain of $ _____ as an (**operating / other**) revenue and the 20X4 statement of cash flows would report a cash (**inflow / outflow**) of $ _____ in the (**operating / investing / financing**) activity section.

5. When available-for-sale securities are sold at a gain, this event will:
   a. (**increase / decrease / have no effect on**) total assets,
   b. (**increase / decrease / have no effect on**) net income,
   c. (**increase / decrease / have no effect on**) comprehensive income, and
   d. (**increase / decrease / have no effect on**) stockholders' equity.

CURRENT and LONG-TERM LIABILITIES

Purpose: · Reinforce understanding of amounts reported on the financial statements for current and long-term liabilities.

12/31/20X5 BALANCE SHEET ACCOUNTS   ($ in millions)

Accounts payable	$6,245
Warranty liability	510
Income taxes payable	389
Current portion of long-term debt	271
Total current liabilities	7,415
Deferred income taxes	51
Post-retirement benefit liabilities	2,390
Bonds payable, 8%, mature in 2010	2,500
Bond discount	(156)
	2,344
Long-term debt	631

20X5 INCOME STATEMENT ACCOUNTS

Net sales revenue	$50,000
Post-retirement benefit expense	698
Warranty expense	275
Interest expense (related to the bond payable)	220

Refer to the information presented above to answer the following questions.

1.   (**Current / Long-term**) liabilities are obligations due within one year or within the company's normal operating cycle if longer. Obligations due beyond that time are classified as (**current / long-term**) liabilities.
2.   The purchase of inventory would increase the _____ account.
3.   Warranty costs related to 20X5 sales total (**$275 / $510 / $785**) million and warranty costs expected to be incurred in the future total (**$275 / $510 / $785**) million. These amounts are (**known / estimated**).

4.   There is (**$271 / $631 / $902**) million of total debt outstanding (not including bonds). Of this amount, the company plans to pay (**$271 / $631 / $902**) million during the following year and pay (**$271 / $631 / $902**) million in later years.

5.   When bonds payable are issued, they are recorded at their (**face / present**) value. After issuance, they are reported at their (**present / fair market / amortized**) value. The above bond has a current carrying value of $_____ million that will continue to (**increase / decrease**) until maturity. At maturity, the issuing corporation will pay $_____ million to the holder of the bond.

6.   The bond payable was issued at a discount because the market interest rates were (**higher than / equal to / lower than**) 8%, and therefore, the actual cost of borrowing is (**greater than / equal to / less than**) 8%. This year's interest payment totaled (**$156 / $200 / $220 / $250**) while this year's cost of borrowing totaled (**$156 / $200 / $220 / $250**).

7.   Post-retirement benefits are expensed and recorded as a liability in the year of (**employment / retirement**). This is an application of the (**matching / cost / reliability**) principle.

STOCKHOLDERS' EQUITY

Purpose: · Reinforce understanding of amounts reported on the financial statements for stockholders' equity.

COCA-COLA COMPANY
December 31, 2002

Share-Owners' Equity	($ in millions)
Common stock, $.25 par value	
Authorized: 5,600,000,000 shares	
Issued: 3,490,818,627 shares in 2002.......................................$ 873	
Capital surplus*...3,857	
Reinvested earnings 24,506	
Accumulated other comprehensive income and	
unearned compensation on restricted stock...................................(3,047)	
Less treasury shares, at cost (1,019,839,490 shares in 2002)..................14,389	

* Assume capital surplus is all from issuing common stock above the par value.

Refer to the financial information above to answer the following questions.

1. The total amount of financing received from shareholders since incorporation is $_____ million and is generally referred to as _____. Common stock of the Coca-Cola Company was originally issued (**above / at / below / can't tell**) par at an average price of $_____ per share.

2. When additional shares of common stock are issued, this event will:
   a. (**increase / decrease / have no effect on**) total assets,
   b. (**increase / decrease / have no effect on**) net income,
   c. (**increase / decrease / have no effect on**) stockholders' equity, and
   d. (**increase / decrease / have no effect on**) earnings per share.

3. The amount of net income retained in the business and not yet distributed as dividends to the shareholders is $_____ million, which is generally referred to as

   _____.

4. Retained earnings (**is / is not**) a reservoir of cash available for dividends.

5. Treasury stock is considered (**issued / outstanding / retired**) but no longer (**issued / outstanding retired**). The average price paid for treasury stock is approximately $_____ per share.

6. When a company buys back its own stock, this event will:
   a. (**increase / decrease / have no effect on**) total assets,
   b. (**increase / decrease / have no effect on**) net income,
   c. (**increase / decrease / have no effect on**) stockholders' equity, and
   d. (**increase / decrease / have no effect on**) earnings per share.

7. The number of common shares currently *outstanding* is #_____ shares, which represents 100% ownership of the company.

8. Total stockholders' equity is $_____ million, which is the amount of business assets owned by shareholders.

9. List several factors that would attract you to purchase shares of stock in a particular corporation.

CURRENT MARKET INTEREST RATES

Purpose: · Benchmark current market rates and understand why they differ among various financial instruments.

1. Research the following current interest rates. These rates are typically reported in the local newspaper or on the Internet and also available by inquiring at a local bank or credit union.

   The current rates banks/credit unions are offering/asking are

   a. _____ %   for a regular savings accounts.

   b. _____ %   for a 2-year certificate of deposit (CD).

   c. _____ %   for a 30-year fixed-rate mortgage with no points.

   d. _____ %   for a credit card.

   Please note the source of your information: _____

   (financial institution, newspaper, website, etc.)

2. The current prime-lending rate is _____%, which is the interest rate charged by banks to their most creditworthy customers (usually the most prominent and stable business customers).

   Please note the source of your information: _____

   (financial institution, newspaper, website, etc.)

3. Explain why the reported interest rates differ between (a) and (b) above.

4. Explain why the reported interest rates differ between (b) and (c) above.

5. Explain why the reported interest rates differ between (c) and (d) above.

6. Explain the prime lending rate and its importance with regard to other lending rates.

EXAMINING BOND YIELDS

Purpose: · Understand why bond yields differ.

YIELD COMPARISONS

CORPORATE BONDS

Maturity	Rating	5/9/03 Yield
1-10 years	High quality (AAA-AA).............	2.95%
1-10 years	Medium quality (A-BBB/Baa).....	3.92%
10+ years	High quality (AAA-AA).............	5.34%
10+ years	Medium quality (A-BBB/Baa).....	5.95%
all years	High yield (BB/Ba-C)	9.23%

Source: *The Wall Street Journal*, Monday, May 12, 2003, p. C13.

NEW TAX-EXEMPT BONDS

Maturity (rating)	5/9/03 Yield
7-12 years G.O. (AA)...............	3.30%
12-22 years G.O. (AA)...............	4.19%
22+ years G.O. (AA)...............	4.70%

Refer to the information in the table above to answer the following questions.

1. <u>Yield</u> is the cost to the issuing entity for borrowing, and the return to the investor/creditor for lending the money. Yield is also referred to as the market rate and the effective rate of borrowing.
    Record the yield of a *high-quality* corporate bond that matures in *1-10 years*. _____%

2. <u>Ratings</u> are a measure of risk. Standard and Poor's and Moody's are two companies that assess the amount of risk. A rating of AAA indicates very low risk, and a rating of C indicates very high risk.
    a. Record the yield of a *high-quality* corporate bond that matures in 1-10 years. _____%
    b. Record the yield of a *high-yield* corporate bond.   _____ %
    c. *Explain* why one yield is higher than the other for these two types of corporate bonds.

3. Bonds have different lengths of <u>time to maturity</u>.
    a. Record the yield of a high-quality corporate bond that *matures in 1-10 years*. _____ %
    b. Record the yield of a high-quality corporate bond that *matures in over 10 years*._____%
    c. *Explain* why one yield is higher than the other for these two types of corporate bonds.

4. Bonds issued by corporations are usually not <u>tax-exempt</u>, while bonds issued by municipalities usually are tax-exempt.
    a. Record the yield of a high-quality *corporate bond* that matures in 10+ years. _____ %
    b. Record the yield of a high-quality *tax-exempt bond* that matures in 7-12 years._____%
    c. *Explain* the advantage of tax-exempt bonds to the investor/creditor.

    d. *Explain* why one yield is higher than the other for these two types of bonds.

EXAMINING THE BOND MARKET

Purpose: · Understand why bonds sell at a premium, at par, or at a discount.

HIGH-YIELD BONDS

Name	Rating	Coupon Rate	Maturity	Bid Price	5/9/03 Yield*
Allied Waste	B+	10.00 %	8/09	104.50	8.71%
Trump AC	CCC+	11.25 %	5/06	79.00	21.13%

* Yield is the lower of yield to maturity and yield to call.
Source: *The Wall Street Journal*, Monday, May 12, 2003, p. C2.

Refer to the information in the table above to answer the following questions.

1. The Allied Waste bond has a _____% coupon rate (also referred to as the stated rate or the face rate) that determines the (**cash interest payment / effective interest rate**). An investor/creditor holding a $100,000 Allied Waste bond will receive $_____ in interest payments each year.

2. The Allied Waste bond is currently rated a B+ and returning a _____% yield, while the Trump AC bond is rated _____ and returning a _____% yield.

   The CCC+ rating indicates (**more / less**) financial risk than a B+ rating. Therefore, to attract investors/creditors the Trump AC bond must offer a (**higher / lower**) rate of return (yield).

3. An investor/creditor purchasing the Allied Waste bond on 5/9/03 is expecting an _____ % annual return. Assuming investments with the same amount of risk, an investor/creditor would prefer a (**high / low**) yield while the issuing corporation would prefer a (**high / low**) yield.

4. The amount paid by the issuing corporation at maturity is referred to as the face value, the par value, and the maturity value. Bond bid (selling) price is quoted as a percentage of par.

   For example, on 5/9/03 the Bid Price of the Allied Waste bond is 104.50. This indicates an investor/creditor could purchase or sell a $100,000 Allied Waste bond for $104,500. ($100,000 x 104.50%). This bond is selling at a (**premium / par / discount**).

   On 5/9/03, a $100,000 Trump AC bond would sell for $_____. This bond is selling at a (**premium / par / discount**).

5. The Allied Waste bond is selling at a premium because the coupon rate (stated rate, face rate) is (**greater than / less than**) the yield (market rate, effective rate) for this investment. To achieve the (**higher / lower**) yield, the investor/creditor pays the issuing corporation an additional amount (premium) at the beginning of the investment.

   The Trump AC bond is selling at a discount because the coupon rate (stated rate, face rate) is (**greater than / less than**) the yield (market rate, effective rate) for this investment. To achieve the (**higher / lower**) yield, the initial investment of the investor/creditor is less than face value (discount) and at maturity the higher face value is received.

6. Would you prefer to invest in the Allied Waste or the Trump AC bond? Why?

Activity 75   **EXAMINING THE DOW JONES INDUSTRIAL AVERAGE**
                         Using The Wall Street Journal

Purpose: · Identify the companies that comprise the Dow Jones Industrial Average (DJIA).
              · Understand how the DJIA is computed.
              · Understand the information provided by the DJIA average.

1. **Companies comprising the Dow Jones Industrial Average (DJIA).** The DJIA is the most quoted
    stock market index. The first DJIA was computed using 30 industrial stocks traded on the New
    York Stock Exchange on October 1, 1928. The 30 corporations comprising the index have
    changed many times to reflect the changing economy.

    In *The Wall Street Journal* find C Section titled "Money & Investing." Find the "Dow 30
    Components" that lists the 30 stocks that currently comprise the Dow Jones Industrial Average
    (DJIA). (*Hint*: Generally located on pages C2 or C3 near the Dow Jones Industrial Average graph.) List six of
    these stocks in the space provided below.

    1. _____   4. _____

    2. _____   5. _____

    3. _____   6. _____

2. **Computing the DJIA.** The index started as a true average of the market values of the stocks
    comprising the index. However, the average computation needed to be adjusted for stock splits and
    stock dividends. On 5/9/2003 the market values are added together and divided by a divisor of
    0.14279922.

    a. On 5/4/2003 if each of the DJIA stocks increased in value by one dollar per share then the
        DJIA would increase by approximately 210 points. (30/.14279922 = 210)

    b. On 5/4/2003 assume the DJIA increased by approximately 420 points. On average, each DJIA
        company would have increased in value by $_____ per share.

    c. The current DJIA divisor is _____. (*Hint*: Generally located on
        pages C2 or C3 near the Dow Jones Industrial Average graph.)

    d. Now, if each of the DJIA stocks increased in value by one dollar the DJIA would increase by
        approximately _____ points. (*Hint*: 30 / current divisor)

    e. Today, assume the DJIA increased by approximately 500 points. On average, each DJIA
        company would have increased in value by $ _____ per share.

    f. When the Dow Jones Industrial Average increases in value, then the majority of stocks traded
        on the New York Stock Exchange would also be expected to (**increase** / decrease).

3. **Historical Summary of the DJIA.** The following chart summarizes the DJIA at various points in history. Using the information presented in the chart, complete the graph outlined below.

Date	DJIA
1928................200
1981.............1,000
1986.............2,000
1991.............3,000
1995.............4,000
1995.............5,000
1996.............6,000
1997.............7,000
1997.............8,000
1998.............9,000
1999...........10,000
1999...........11,000

Current information:

_____   _____

```
13,000 |                              DJIA
12,000 |
11,000 |
10,000 |
 9,000 |
 8,000 |
 7,000 |
 6,000 |
 5,000 |
 4,000 |
 3,000 |
 2,000 |
 1,000 |_____
        1928  '38  '48  '58  '68   '81  '91  2001
```

4. In *The Wall Street Journal*, refer to the "Markets Diary" section generally found on page C1 to record the information requested below.

   a. The DJIA closed at _____ points on _____ (date).

   b. In #3 above, update the chart and graph with the DJIA closing information just recorded.

5. Over the years the DJIA has had its ups and downs, but since 1928 the general direction of the DJIA has been (**increasing / decreasing**).

   a. *Comment* on the significance of this trend to investors.

   b. *Comment* on the significance of this trend to corporations.

HOW TO READ STOCK QUOTES
Using the Wall Street Journal

Purpose: · Locate and understand the stock quote information reported in *The Wall Street Journal*.

1. Use a current issue of *The Wall Street Journal* to answer the following questions.

   At the bottom of page A1 find *"Today's Contents."*
   Record the page numbers where the following information is located.
   a. **NYSE Stocks** are on page _____.
   b. **Nasdaq Stocks** are on page _____.

2. a. Look at NYSE Stocks. Use the **"New York Stock Exchange Composite Transactions"** section to record the information requested for the three companies listed below.

Company	YTD %Chg	52 Weeks Hi	Lo	Stock Sym	Div	Yld %	PE	Vol 100s	Close	Net Chg
AOL Time Warner	__	__	__	AOL	__	__	__	__	__	__
Berkshire Hathaway	__	__	__	BRKA	__	__	__	__	__	__
Disney	__	__	__	DIS	__	__	__	__	__	__

   b. Find the **How To Read This Table** for the New York Stock Exchange Composite Transactions (generally on page C3).

      1. This information is located on page _____.

      2. The column titled **"Div"** reports (**monthly / quarterly / annual**) dividend distributions.

      3. A footnote of **"s"** indicates (**selling price / a stock split or stock dividend**).

   c. Refer to the information reported above to answer the following questions.
      1. For **AOL Time Warner**, the highest market price reported in the past 52 weeks was $_____ per share and the closing market price was $_____ per share.

      2. For **Berkshire Hathaway**, the last price traded was $_____ per share and only _____ shares were traded.

      3. During the past year, **Disney** distributed a dividend of $_____ per share, which is _____% of the current market price per share. A Disney shareholder is willing to pay _____ times earnings for one share of stock.

Activity 77   **FOLLOWING THE STOCK MARKET**
Using The Wall Street Journal or the Internet

Purpose: · Follow the stock market quotes for three companies and the Dow Jones Industrial Average (DJIA) for four weeks.
                 · Understand market value per share.

1. Select three corporations. For each of the next four weeks record in the chart below the (a) date of the stock information, (b) the closing stock price of the three companies you selected, and (c) the DJIA as of the close (end) of that business day.

   Stock quote information can be found in *The Wall Street Journal*, other newspapers reporting stock market quotes, or on the Internet. Note: Activity 106, *Market Research*, introduces a website with stock quote information.

Corporation Name	Company #1	Company #2	Company #3	DJIA
WEEK ONE: Closing Market Price on _____ (a)				
WEEK TWO: Closing Market Price on _____				
WEEK THREE: Closing Market Price on _____				
WEEK FOUR: Closing Market Price on _____ (b)				
Four week change in market price (b) - (a)				
Four week % change in market price (b - a) / (a)	%	%	%	%

2. *At the end of the four weeks* complete the following:
   a. Compute the information requested in the bottom two rows of the above chart.

   b. Over the four weeks you observed the DJIA (**increased / stayed the same / decreased**).

   c. Did the stocks you selected move in the same direction as the Dow Jones Industrial Average? (**Yes / No**)

   d. Would you expect your stocks to move in the same direction as the DJIA? (**Yes / No**) *Explain* why.

   e. *Comment* on at least two interesting results you noted while following the stock market.

CHAPTER 7

COMPREHENSIVE REVIEW

PURPOSE: Chapter 7 provides a comprehensive review of the major financial statements. The activities review understanding of transaction analysis, identifying specific account information, interpreting financial information, and a comprehensive analysis of three well-known companies.

QUESTION: **When using LIFO, the most recent (current) inventory costs are reported on which financial statement?** Read this chapter to find the answer.

CORPORATIONS FEATURED

Lucent Technologies Inc. (LU NYSE) is a global leader in telecom equipment that manufactures products used to build communications network infrastructure. The company also makes communications and network management software and provides a wide range of services. Many of Lucent's products are developed by its Bell Laboratories research and development unit. The company provides wireline and wireless products to leading telephone companies and other communications service providers. Former parent AT&T is a major customer. www.lucent.com

Royal Caribbean Cruises Ltd. (RCL NYSE) is the world's second-largest cruise line (behind Carnival) providing cruises in Alaska, the Caribbean, and Europe on 25 different cruise ships. The firm's two cruise brands, Celebrity Cruises and Royal Caribbean International, carry over two million passengers a year to about 200 destinations. www.rccl.com

----
Numerous sources including *Hoover's Company Capsules*, **Hoover's, Inc., 2003.**

TRANSACTIONS AFFECTING TOTAL ASSETS

Purpose: · Review the effect of various transactions on total assets.

Circle whether each of the following events/transactions will (**I**)ncrease, (**D**)ecrease, or have (**No**) effect on *total assets*.

		<u>TOTAL ASSETS</u> Circle the answer
a.	Purchase equipment on account.	(**I / D / No**)
b.	Purchase supplies for cash.	(**I / D / No**)
c.	Record depreciation for the equipment.	(**I / D / No**)
d.	Sell equipment at a gain for cash.	(**I / D / No**)
e.	Record a cash sale to customer ABC.	(**I / D / No**)
f.	Record a sale on account to customer XYZ.	(**I / D / No**)
g.	Record the receipt of cash from customer XYZ in (f).	(**I / D / No**)
h.	Purchase short-term trading securities for cash.	(**I / D / No**)
i.	At the end of the accounting period, the short-term trading securities purchased in (h) have increased in market value.	(**I / D / No**)
j.	Land purchased ten years ago has increased in market value.	(**I / D / No**)
k.	The current market value of high-tech inventory is less than acquisition cost.	(**I / D / No**)
l.	Issue a bond payable at a discount for cash.	(**I / D / No**)
m.	Purchase treasury stock for cash.	(**I / D / No**)
n.	Pay a cash dividend.	(**I / D / No**)

Activity 79   **TRANSACTIONS AFFECTING TOTAL LIABILITIES**

Purpose: · Review the effect of various transactions on total liabilities.

Circle whether each of the following events/transactions will (**I**)ncrease, (**D**)ecrease, or have (**No**) effect on *total liabilities*.

		TOTAL LIABILITIES Circle the answer
a.	Purchase inventory on account.	(**I** / **D** / **No**)
b.	Pay for the inventory purchased in (a).	(**I** / **D** / **No**)
c.	Hire a new employee for an annual salary of $20,000. The employee will start next Monday.	(**I** / **D** / **No**)
d.	Issue bond payable at a discount.	(**I** / **D** / **No**)
e.	Note payable is paid in full before the due date without penalty.	(**I** / **D** / **No**)
f.	Retirement costs for current employees are recorded. These costs will not be paid until an employee retires in a future accounting period.	(**I** / **D** / **No**)
g.	The end of the accounting period is on a Wednesday. Record accrued employee wage expense. Employees will get paid on Friday.	(**I** / **D** / **No**)
h.	At the end of the accounting period, record accrued interest expense on a note payable.	(**I** / **D** / **No**)
i.	At the end of the accounting period, estimate the amount of income taxes owed for the fiscal year.	(**I** / **D** / **No**)
j.	Company ABC files a lawsuit. Company lawyers evaluate the case and estimate the company will *probably win* a substantial amount for damages. The case will be tried in a future accounting period.	(**I** / **D** / **No**)
k.	A lawsuit is filed against Company ABC. Company lawyers evaluate the case and estimate the company will *probably lose and owe* a substantial amount for damages. The case will be tried in a future accounting period.	(**I** / **D** / **No**)

Activity 80   **TRANSACTIONS AFFECTING TOTAL STOCKHOLDERS' EQUITY**

Purpose: · Review the effect of various transactions on total stockholders' equity.

Circle whether each of the following events/transactions will **(I)**ncrease, **(D)**ecrease, or have **(No)** effect on *total stockholders' equity*.

<u>TOTAL STOCKHOLDERS' EQUITY</u>
Circle the answer

a. Issue preferred stock at par value.   **(I / D / No)**

b. Purchase inventory on account.   **(I / D / No)**

c. Issue bonds payable at a premium.   **(I / D / No)**

d. Declare and issue a *cash* dividend.   **(I / D / No)**

e. Declare and issue a *stock* dividend.   **(I / D / No)**

f. Purchase treasury stock.   **(I / D / No)**

g. During the accounting period, the market price of the
    corporation's common stock increases.   **(I / D / No)**

h. Record net income for the accounting period.   **(I / D / No)**

i. Correct an error that resulted in understating
    depreciation expense in the previous accounting period.   **(I / D / No)**

TRANSACTIONS AFFECTING NET INCOME

Purpose: · Review the effect of various transactions on net income.

Circle whether each of the following events/transactions will **(I)**ncrease, **(D)**ecrease, or have **(No)** effect on *net income*.

NET INCOME
Circle the answer

a. Record a sale for customer ABC paying cash.   **(I / D / No)**

b1. Record a sale for customer DEF on account.   **(I / D / No)**
b2. Record cash received from customer DEF for the sale recorded in (b1). **(I / D / No)**

c1. Purchase equipment.   **(I / D / No)**
c2. At the end of the accounting period, make the adjusting entry
      to record depreciation for the equipment.   **(I / D / No)**
c3. Record a loss on the sale of equipment.   **(I / D / No)**

d1. Borrow $10,000 from the bank and sign a note.   **(I / D / No)**
d2. At the end of the accounting period, make the adjusting entry
      to record accrued interest expense on the note in (d1).   **(I / D / No)**
d3. Repay the $10,000 note.   **(I / D / No)**

e. Pay rent for this accounting period.   **(I / D / No)**

f. Record an extraordinary gain.   **(I / D / No)**

g. Declare and issue a cash dividend.   **(I / D / No)**

h. Issue common stock for more than the par value.   **(I / D / No)**

i. At the end of the accounting period, record the portion of sales
     estimated as uncollectible.   **(I / D / No)**

j. At the end of the accounting period, record an unrealized gain
     on the short-term trading securities portfolio.   **(I / D / No)**

k. Change the accounting method
     from the double-declining-balance (DDB) depreciation method
     to the straight-line depreciation method.   **(I / D / No)**

WHICH FINANCIAL STATEMENT?

Purpose: · Reinforce understanding of the information provided by each financial statement.

Circle the financial statement you would consult to find the following information.
If more than one answer is correct, circle only one financial statement.

> **BS** = Balance sheet
> **IS** = Income statement
> **RE** = Statement of retained earnings
> **CF** = Statement of cash flows
> **Not** = Not found on any of the financial statements

Circle only one correct answer

a. Rental costs incurred this year. **(BS/IS/RE/CF/Not)**

b. Rental costs paid this year. **(BS/IS/RE/CF/Not)**

c. Rental costs still owed. **(BS/IS/RE/CF/Not)**

d. Cost of equipment allocated to this accounting period. **(BS/IS/RE/CF/Not)**

e. Equipment book value (carrying value). **(BS/IS/RE/CF/Not)**

f. Current market value of equipment purchased ten years ago. **(BS/IS/RE/CF/Not)**

g. Accrual-basis accounting used to compute operating results. **(BS/IS/RE/CF/Not)**

h. Cash-basis accounting used to compute operating results. **(BS/IS/RE/CF/Not)**

i. Noncash investing and financing activities. **(BS/IS/RE/CF/Not)**

j. Market value of investments in the short-term trading portfolio. **(BS/IS/RE/CF/Not)**

k. Unrealized gain on the short-term investment portfolio. **(BS/IS/RE/CF/Not)**

l. Market value of the common stock issued by the corporation. **(BS/IS/RE/CF/Not)**

m. Amounts contributed by common shareholders. **(BS/IS/RE/CF/Not)**

n. Inventory remaining unsold at the end of the accounting period. **(BS/IS/RE/CF/Not)**

o. Inventory sold during the accounting period. **(BS/IS/RE/CF/Not)**

p. If we use the FIFO inventory cost flow assumption, the
most current inventory costs will end up on this statement. **(BS/IS/RE/CF/Not)**

q. Evaluate how assets are currently being financed. **(BS/IS/RE/CF/Not)**

r. Financial statement reporting amounts as of a certain date. **(BS/IS/RE/CF/Not)**

FINANCIAL STATEMENT PREPARATION

Purpose: · Apply the revenue recognition and the matching principles.
                · Differentiate between accrual accounting and cash accounting.
                · Prepare a multi-step income statement, the statement of retained earnings, a classified balance sheet, and the operating activity section of the statement of cash flows.

Betty opened Books Galore, Inc., for business on January 1, 20X1. The following financial items summarize the first year of operations. Use these items to prepare the 20X1 multi-step income statement, the 20X1 statement of retained earnings, the 12/31/20X1 classified balance sheet, and the operating activity section of the 20X1 statement of cash flows in the space provided.

a.   Betty and her friend each invested $50,000 in cash (for a total of $100,000) in exchange for shares of common stock in Books Galore, Inc.

b.   On January 1, 20X1, purchased new equipment costing $70,000 with a 10-year useful life and no residual value. Paid cash. Straight-line depreciation is used.

c.   Rental costs for the year total $48,000. Of that amount, $4,000 remains unpaid on 12/31/20X1.

d.   Purchased and paid $2,000 for a two-year property insurance policy.

e.   On January 1, 20X1, purchased a piece of land next to the store for $20,000 in cash. Later in the year, the land was sold to another small business owner for $30,000 in cash.

f.   During 20X1, customers purchased $300,000 of books. Of that amount, $250,000 has been collected from customers in cash and the remaining amounts will be collected next year.

g.   Inventory purchases totaled $200,000 for the year. All purchases have been paid for, and $18,000 of those purchases remains in inventory at the end of the year.

h.   On July 1, 20X1, borrowed $25,000 from a local bank and signed a one-year, 10% note payable. Principal and interest are due on June 30, 20X2.

i.   The company paid shareholders cash dividends totaling $8,000.

j.   At the end of the year, adjusting entries were recorded for depreciation expense and interest expense.

20X1 Multi-Step Income Statement
For the Year Ended 12/31/20X1

Sales revenue
Cost of goods sold
Gross margin
Operating expenses:

Other gains and losses:

Net income

Statement of Retained Earnings
For the Year Ended 12/31/20X1

Classified Balance Sheet
12/31/20X1

CURRENT ASSETS

CURRENT LIABILITIES

PROPERTY, PLANT, AND EQUIPMENT

STOCKHOLDERS' EQUITY

Statement Of Cash Flows
For the Year Ended 12/31/20X1
(Prepare using the direct method.)

Cash flows from operating activities:
Receipts:

Payments:

Net cash inflow from operating activities

TEST YOUR UNDERSTANDING
Comprehensive Analysis

Purpose: · Analyze the income statement, the balance sheet, and the statement of cash flows.
· Prepare a statement of retained earnings.

ROYAL CARIBBEAN CRUISES
Balance Sheet

($ in millions)	12/31/2002	12/31/2001	12/31/2000	12/31/1999
Cash	$ 243	$ 727	$ 178	$ 64
Receivables	80	72	54	53
Inventories	37	33	30	26
Prepaid expenses	88	54	49	51
Total current assets	448	886	311	194
Property, plant, and equipment, net	9,277	8,605	6,832	5,858
Intangibles	277	279	289	299
Deposits and other long-term assets	537	599	397	30
TOTAL assets	$10,539	$10,369	$7,829	$6,381
Accounts payable	$ 171	$ 144	$ 158	$ 103
Accrued expenses	308	284	201	209
Current portion of long-term debt	123	239	110	128
Other current liabilities	568	446	444	465
Total current liabilities	1,170	1,113	913	905
Long-term debt	5,322	5,408	3,300	2,214
Other long-term liabilities	12	91	-0-	-0-
Total liabilities	6,504	6,612	4,213	3,119
Preferred stock	-0-	0	0	172
Common stock, par	2	2	2	2
Additional paid-in capital	2,054	2,045	2,043	1,877
Retained earnings	1,983	1,732	1,577	1,216
Treasury stock and other equity	(4)	(22)	(6)	(5)
TOTAL liabilities and stockholders' equity	$10,539	$10,369	$7,829	$6,381

ROYAL CARIBBEAN CRUISES
Income Statement

($ in millions)	2002	2001	2000	1999
Revenues	$3,434	$3,145	$2,866	$2,546
Cost of revenues	2,113	1,934	1,653	1,496
Gross margin	1,321	1,211	1,213	1,050
Selling, general, and administrative expenses	431	454	413	372
Depreciation and amortization expense	339	301	231	198
Interest expense	267	253	154	131
Nonoperating income (loss)	+67	+52	+30	+35
Net income	$ 351	$ 255	$ 455	$ 384
Basic earnings per share	$1.825	$1.324	$2.341	$2.155

ROYAL CARIBBEAN CRUISES
Statement of Cash Flows

($ in millions)	2002	2001	2000	1999
CASH FLOWS FROM OPERATING ACTIVITIES				
Net income (loss)	$ 351	$ 255	$ 445	$ 383
Depreciation/amortization expense	339	301	231	198
Net increase (decrease) in assets/liabilities	133	42	27	2
Other adjustments, net	48	36	-0-	-0-
Net cash inflows (outflows) from operating activities	871	634	703	583
CASH FLOWS FROM INVESTING ACTIVITIES				
(Increase) decrease in property, plant, and equipment	(690)	(1,737)	(1,286)	(972)
Other cash inflow (outflow)	(6)	(47)	(279)	(15)
Net cash inflows (outflows) from investing activities	(696)	(1,784)	(1,565)	(987)
CASH FLOWS FROM FINANCING ACTIVITIES				
Issue (purchase) of equity	-0-	-0-	-0-	487
Increase (decrease) in borrowing	(603)	1,789	1,067	(128)
Dividends	(100)	(100)	(94)	(82)
Other cash inflows (outflows)	44	10	3	18
Net cash inflows (outflows) from financing activities	(659)	1,699	976	295
Net change in cash equivalents	(484)	549	114	(109)
Cash equivalents at year start	727	178	64	173
Cash equivalents at year end	$ 243	$ 727	$ 178	$ 64

Refer to the financial statements presented for Royal Caribbean Cruises on the previous two pages to answer the following questions.

BALANCE SHEET

1. (1) Examine the following accounts, subtotals, and totals; (2) describe your observations; and then (3) identify what your observations indicate. A response is given for PPE, net to help with understanding.

   a. Property, plant, and equipment, net ... *increased by 58% from 12/31/1999 to 12/31/2002 with the greatest increase during 2001, indicating purchases of additional cruise ships for expansion.*

   b. Long-term debt ...

   c. For 2002, contributed capital totals $_____ million and stockholders' equity totals
   $_____ million.

   d. Total contributed capital ...

   e. Retained earnings ...

2. Compute the <u>current ratio</u> (current assets / current liabilities) for each year and *comment* on what the results indicate.

3. Compute the <u>debt ratio</u> (total liabilities / total assets) for each year and *comment* on what the results indicate.

4. Review the four years of information reported on the balance sheet and *comment* on your observations.

INCOME STATEMENT

5. <u>Revenues</u> were $_____ million for the earliest year reported and $_____ million for the most recent year reported. Since the earliest year reported, this account has (**increased / decreased**) by $_____ million, which is a _____% (**increase / decrease**). During the same time period, <u>net income</u> (**increased / decreased**) by _____ %.

6. Compute the <u>gross margin percentage</u> (gross margin / revenues) for each year. The strongest gross margin percentage was reported in (**2002 / 2001 / 2000 / 1999**). *Comment* on the results.

7. Compute the <u>return-on-sales</u> ratio (net income / revenues) for each year. The strongest return on sales was reported in (**2002 / 2001 / 2000 / 1999**). *Comment* on the results.

8. Review the four years of information reported on the income statement and *comment* on your observations.

STATEMENT OF CASH FLOWS

9. The primary source of cash:

    in 1999 was (**operating / investing / financing**).

    in 2000 was (**operating / investing / financing**), which was primarily the result of

        (**borrowing / issuing stock / selling PPE**).

    in 2001 was (**operating / investing / financing**), which was primarily the result of

        (**borrowing / issuing stock / selling PPE**).

    in 2002 was (**operating / investing / financing**).

10. Cash from operating activities reported a cash (**inflow / outflow**) all four years, which is a(n) (**favorable / unfavorable**) sign.

11. For property, plant, and equipment, in each of the past four years a net cash (**inflow / outflow**) was reported in the (**operating / investing / financing**) activity section indicating PPE was (**purchased / sold**). This is a(n) (**favorable / unfavorable**) sign *indicating* …

12. For equities, in 1999 a net cash (**inflow / outflow**) was reported in the (**operating / investing / financing**) activity section indicating common stock was (**issued / purchased**). This is a(n) (**favorable / unfavorable**) sign *indicating* …

13. Borrowing during (**2002 / 2001 / 2000 / 1999**) resulted in a net cash (**inflow / outflow**). These borrowed amounts appear to have financed (**operations / the purchase of PPE / the purchase of common stock / dividend payments**).

STATEMENT OF RETAINED EARNINGS

14. Identify net income reported in the following years: 2002 $_____ million, 2001 $_____ million, and 2000 $_____ million. Net income is initially reported on the (**balance sheet / income statement / statement of cash flows**).

15. Identify dividends paid in the following years: 2002 $_____ million, 2001 $_____ million, and 2000 $_____ million. Dividends paid are reported on the (**balance sheet / income statement / statement of cash flows**).

16. Prepare a statement of retained earnings for: <u>   2002   </u>   <u>   2001   </u>   <u>   2000   </u>

OTHER

17. Royal Caribbean Cruises competes within the (**entertainment / Internet / semiconductor**) industry.

18. Based on the financial statements presented for Royal Caribbean Cruises, comment on whether you would invest in this company. *Support* your response with at least two good observations.

TEST YOUR UNDERSTANDING
Comprehensive Analysis

Purpose: · Analyze the income statement, the balance sheet, and the statement of cash flows.
· Prepare a statement of retained earnings.

LUCENT TECHNOLOGIES INC.
Balance Sheet

($ in millions)	9/30/2002	9/30/2001	9/30/2000	9/30/1999
Cash and cash equivalents	$ 2,894	$ 2,390	$ 1,467	$ 1,686
Short-term investments	1,526	-0-	-0-	-0-
Receivables	1,647	4,594	8,782	8,799
Inventories	1,363	3,646	5,100	4,240
Other current assets	1,725	5,473	5,191	4,515
Total current assets	9,155	16,103	20,540	19,240
Property, plant, and equipment, net	1,977	4,416	5,046	6,219
Goodwill and other intangibles	224	1,466	6,463	1,396
Other long-term assets	6,435	11,679	15,463	8,517
TOTAL assets	$17,791	$33,664	$47,512	$35,372
Accounts payable	1,298	1,844	2,583	2,537
Accrued expenses	1,094	1,500	1,010	1,788
Current portion of long-term debt	120	1,135	3,468	1,705
Other current liabilities	3,814	5,690	3,099	3,120
Total current liabilities	6,326	10,169	10,160	9,150
Long-term debt	3,236	3,274	3,030	4,162
Other long-term liabilities	11,283	7,364	8,150	8,124
Total long-term liabilities	14,519	10,638	11,180	12,286
TOTAL liabilities	20,845	20,807	21,340	21,436
Preferred stock, redeemable	1,680	1,834	-0-	-0-
Common stock, par	35	34	34	31
Additional paid-in capital	20,606	21,702	20,374	7,994
Retained earnings	(22,025)	(10,272)	6,130	6,188
Other equity	(3,350)	(441)	(366)	(277)
TOTAL equity	(3,054)	12,857	26,172	13,936
TOTAL liabilities and stockholders' equity	$17,791	$33,664	$47,512	$35,372

LUCENT TECHNOLOGIES INC.
Income Statement

($ in millions) Fiscal year ended September 30	2002	2001	2000	1999
Revenues	$12,321	$21,294	$28,904	$26,993
Cost of revenues	10,705	18,036	17,190	14,024
Gross margin	1,616	3,258	11,714	12,969
Selling, general, and administrative expenses	2,466	4,240	4,743	5,371
Research and development	2,310	3,520	3,179	3,536
Depreciation and amortization expense	250	921	362	-0-
Unusual expense (income)	2,034	11,591	196	276
Other operating expenses	1,253	2,249	505	-0-
Interest expense	382	518	342	318
Other nonoperating gains (losses)	+10	(123)	(30)	+357
Income from continuing operations before tax	(7,069)	(19,904)	2,357	3,825
Provision for income taxes	4,757	(5,734)	924	1,456
Income before nonrecurring items	(11,826)	(14,170)	1,433	2,369
Discontinued operations	73	(3,172)	(214)	1,112
Extraordinary items	-0-	1,182	-0-	-0-
Cumulative effect of change in accounting principle	-0-	(38)	-0-	1,308
Net income	$ (11,753)	$ (16,198)	$ 1,219	$ 4,789

Statement of Cash Flows

($ in millions) Fiscal year ended September 30	2002	2001	2000	1999
CASH FLOWS FROM OPERATING ACTIVITIES				
Net income (loss)	$(11,753)	$(16,198)	$1,219	$4,789
Depreciation/amortization expense	1,470	2,536	1,667	1,282
Net increase (decrease) in assets/liabilities	2,131	3,201	(5,348)	(6,441)
Other adjustments, net	7,396	6,804	1,563	(1,413)
Net cash inflows (outflows) from operating activities	(756)	(3,657)	(899)	(1,783)
CASH FLOWS FROM INVESTING ACTIVITIES				
(Increase) decrease in property, plant, and equipment	(255)	(1,213)	(1,889)	(1,309)
Disposition of business and manufacturing operations	2,576	3,187	276	16
Other investing cash inflow (outflow)	(1,564)	(23)	54	227
Net cash inflows (outflows) from investing activities	757	1,951	(1,559)	(1,066)
CASH FLOWS FROM FINANCING ACTIVITIES				
Issue (purchase) of equity	64	2,053	1,444	725
Increase (decrease) in borrowing	(1,151)	901	1,040	2,887
Dividends	(149)	(204)	(255)	(222)
Other financing cash inflows (outflows)	1,704	(125)	-0-	(40)
Net cash inflows (outflows) from financing activities	468	2,625	2,229	3,350
Foreign exchange effects	35	4	10	41
Net change in cash equivalents	504	923	(219)	542
Cash equivalents at year start	2,390	1,467	1,686	1,144
Cash equivalents at year end	$2,894	$2,390	$1,467	$1,686

Refer to the financial statements presented for Lucent Technologies Inc. on the previous two pages to answer the following questions.

BALANCE SHEET

1. (1) Examine the following accounts, subtotals, and totals; (2) describe your observations; and then (3) identify what your observations indicate. A response is given for PPE, net to help with understanding.

   a. Total assets ... *of $17,791 million on 9/30/2002 are approximately half of the $35,372 million of assets reported on 9/30/1999, indicating the company has gone through a major contraction.*

   b. Total liabilities ...

   c. On 9/30/1999 contributed capital totaled $_____ million and on 9/30/2002 contributed capital totaled $_____ million.   Total contributed capital ...

   d. Retained earnings ...

2. Compute the <u>current ratio</u> (current assets / current liabilities) for each year and *comment* on what the results indicate.

3. Compute the <u>debt ratio</u> (total liabilities / total assets) for each year and *comment* on what the results indicate.

4. Review the four years of information reported on the balance sheet and *comment* on your observations.

INCOME STATEMENT

5. <u>Revenues</u> were $_____ million for the earliest year reported and $_____ million for the most recent year reported. Since the earliest year reported, this account has (**increased / decreased**) by $_____ million, which is a _____% (**increase / decrease**). During the same time period, <u>net income</u> (**dipped / plunged**).

6. Compute the <u>gross margin percentage</u> (gross margin / revenues) for each year. The strongest gross margin percentage was reported during (**2002 / 2001 / 2000 / 1999**). *Comment* on the results.

7. Compute the <u>return-on-sales</u> ratio (net income / revenues) for each year. The strongest return on sales was reported during (**2002 / 2001 / 2000 / 1999**) and the weakest in (**2002 / 2001 / 2000 / 1999**).

8. Review the four years of information reported on the income statement and *comment* on your observations.

STATEMENT OF CASH FLOWS

9. Cash from operating activities reported a cash (**inflow / outflow**) all four years, which is a(n) (**favorable / unfavorable**) sign.

10. The primary source of cash:
    in 1999 was (**operating / investing / financing**), which was primarily the result of (**borrowing / issuing stock / disposing of businesses**).
    in 2000 was (**operating / investing / financing**), which was primarily the result of (**borrowing / issuing stock / disposing of businesses**).
    in 2001 was (**operating / investing / financing**), which was primarily the result of (**borrowing / issuing stock / disposing of businesses**).
    in 2002 was (**operating / investing / financing**), which was primarily the result of (**borrowing / issuing stock / disposing of businesses**).

11. There was a net cash *outflow* reported for operating activities, but *net income* reported on the income statement during (**2002 / 2001 / 2000 / 1999**). This indicates …

12. For investing activities, during (**2002 / 2001 / 2000 / 1999**) a net cash inflow was reported indicating assets were (**purchased / sold**). This is a(n) (**favorable / unfavorable**) sign *indicating* …

13. Equities were issued during (**2002 / 2001 / 2000 / 1999**) resulting in a net cash (**inflow / outflow**), which appears to have financed (**operations / paying back borrowed amounts**).

14. Amounts were borrowed during (**2002 / 2001 / 2000 / 1999**) resulting in a net cash (**inflow / outflow**), which appears to have financed (**operations / the purchase of common stock**).

STATEMENT OF RETAINED EARNINGS

15. Net income reported for the fye 2001 totals $_____ million and is initially reported on the (**balance sheet / income statement / statement of cash flows**). Dividends paid during fye 2001 total $_____ million and are initially reported on the (**balance sheet / income statement / statement of cash flows**). Beginning and ending amounts for retained earnings are initially reported on the (**balance sheet / income statement / statement of cash flows**). Reconcile beginning and ending retained earnings for fiscal year ended September 30, 2001:

OTHER

16. Lucent Technologies Inc. competes within the (**entertainment / Internet / telecom**) industry.

17. Based on the financial statements presented for Lucent Technologies Inc., comment on whether you would invest in this company. *Support* your response with at least two good observations.

CHAPTER 8

EXCEL SPREADSHEET APPLICATIONS

PURPOSE: Chapter 8 introduces the use of Excel spreadsheets for analysis. Excel is used to prepare condensed financial statements, common-size statements, trend percentages, ratios, and graphs. These activities prepare the student for the analysis required to complete the capstone project in Chapter 10.

QUESTION: Did revenues or net income increase at a greater rate for the Fuji Photo Film Co., Ltd since 3/31/99? Read this chapter to find the answer.

FEATURED CORPORATIONS

Eastman Kodak Company (EK NYSE) remains the world's #1 maker of photographic film (ahead of Fuji Photo Film) and continues to devote resources to digital imaging media and other products for both amateur and professional photographers. Kodak also makes film, paper, and processing equipment for professionals in the health care and entertainment industries. Currently, international sales slightly exceed domestic. Trying to remain competitive, Kodak has reduced costs and sold operations such as its copier unit. www.kodak.com

Fuji Photo Film Co., Ltd. (FUJIY Nasdaq) is Japan's #1 photographic film and paper producer. Recently, it has been gaining market share from rival Eastman Kodak and now the two are virtually tied in the global market. The company's principal businesses are imaging systems, information solutions, and document solutions. Increased revenues reflect increased sales on new products, new services, and networks. Fuji has operations in Europe, Australia, Asia, and North and South America, although most of its sales come from Japan. www.fujifilm.co.jp.com

----

Numerous sources including *Hoover's Company Capsules*, Hoover's, Inc., 2003.

Activity 86   **PREPARING CONDENSED BALANCE SHEETS**

Purpose: · Use an Excel spreadsheet to prepare condensed balance sheets.
· Understand and interpret amounts reported on the balance sheet.

1. Open a new Excel file and name it "I&A Ch8."

2. Enter your name in cell A1, today's date in cell A2, and your instructor's name and course in cell A3. Then format as follows:

	A	B	C	D	E
5	**FUJI PHOTO FILM Co., LTD**		**BALANCE**	**SHEETS**	
6					
7	**ASSETS ($ in millions)**	**3/31/02**	**3/31/01**	**3/31/00**	**3/31/99**
8	Current assets	11,598	11,854	11,753	10,687
9	Property, plant, and equipment, net	6,068	5,693	3,787	3,954
10	Other assets	*Formula 1*	*Formula 1*	*Formula 1*	*Formula 1*
11	TOTAL ASSETS	24,598	23,629	18,667	17,695
12					
13	**LIABILITIES**				
14	Current liabilities	6,018	6,745	4,105	3,729
15	Long-term liabilities	*Formula 2*	*Formula 2*	*Formula 2*	*Formula 2*
16	Total liabilities	10,422	10,064	5,516	5,568
17					
18	**STOCKHOLDERS' EQUITY**				
19	Common stock	906	906	906	906
20	Retained earnings	13,510	12,939	12,051	11,300
21	Other stockholders' equity	*Formula 5*	*Formula 5*	*Formula 5*	*Formula 5*
22	Total stockholders' equity	*Formula 4*	*Formula 4*	*Formula 4*	*Formula 4*
23					
24	TOTAL L AND SE	*Formula 3*	*Formula 3*	*Formula 3*	*Formula 3*

3. In column B, prepare the cell formulas in the order designated.
   a. For Formula #1, total assets minus current assets minus property, plant, and equipment, net will equal the amount for other assets. The resulting cell formula is "=+B11-B8-B9". This formula can be typed into cell B10 or the click method may be used. Click on cell B10 and type "=" then click on cell B11 and type "-" and then click on cell B8 and type "-" and then click on cell B9 and hit enter. (*Note*: Quotation marks are not to be typed as part of the cell formulas.)
   b. Prepare the remaining formulas in the order designated.

4. Copy formulas to the other three columns.
   a. To copy Formula #1, highlight cell B10. Select Edit, Copy. Highlight cells C10..E10. Select Edit, Paste.
   b. Copy the remaining formulas to the other three columns.

5. Format numerical amounts.
   a. Highlight B8..E24 for formatting.
   b. Select Format, Cells, and Number. Make the following selections: "Category:" choose Number, "Decimal Places:" choose 0, "Negative numbers:" choose (1,234). Then click OK at the bottom of the screen.

6. Title this first worksheet "Balance Sheet."
   a. Double click on the "Sheet1" tab at the bottom of the screen.
   b. Type in "Balance Sheet" and hit enter.

7. Save the file by selecting File, Save As…, and then name your file "I&A Ch8."

8. Print a copy of your file by selecting File, Print…, and click on *OK*.

9. Review the amounts reported on the balance sheets.
   a. Property, plant, and equipment, net increased by approximately 50% during the fiscal year ending (**3-31-02 / 3-31-01 / 3-31-00**).

   b. The purchase of property, plant, and equipment appears to be primarily financed by (**liabilities / equity**).

   c. Does this company appear to be profitable?   (**Yes / No**)   How can you tell?

   d. This company appears to report a (**strong / weak**) financial position. *Support* your response with at least two observations.

Activity 87   **PREPARING COMMON-SIZE BALANCE SHEETS**

Purpose: · Use an Excel spreadsheet to prepare common-size balance sheets.
                      · Understand and interpret amounts reported on common-size balance sheets.

1. Complete Activity 86. Open the Excel file "I&A Ch8" that was created in Activity 86.
2. Copy the balance sheets created in Activity 86 (cells A5..E24) to a new location starting with cell A30.
3. Highlight B33..E49 for formatting. Select Format, Cells, and Number. Make the following selections: "Category:" choose Percentage, "Decimal Places:" choose 1. Then click *OK*. Results will not make any sense, but that will be corrected as we continue.

	A	B	C	D	E
30	**FUJI PHOTO FILM Co., LTD**	**COMMON-SIZE BALANCE SHEETS**			
31					
32	**ASSETS**	**3/31/02**	**3/31/01**	**3/31/00**	**3/31/99**
33	Current assets	Formula	Copy	Copy	Copy
34	Property, plant, and equipment, net	Formula	Copy	Copy	Copy
35	Other assets	Formula	Copy	Copy	Copy
36	TOTAL ASSETS	Sum Assets	Copy	Copy	Copy
37					
38	**LIABILITIES**				
39	Current liabilities	Formula	Copy	Copy	Copy
40	Long-term liabilities	Formula	Copy	Copy	Copy
41	Total liabilities	Sum Liab	Copy	Copy	Copy
42					
43	**STOCKHOLDERS' EQUITY**				
44	Common stock	Formula	Copy	Copy	Copy
45	Retained earnings	Formula	Copy	Copy	Copy
46	Other stockholders' equity	Formula	Copy	Copy	Copy
47	Total stockholders' equity	Sum SE	Copy	Copy	Copy
48					
49	TOTAL L AND SE	Sum L + SE	Copy	Copy	Copy

4. Common-size statements are a form of vertical analysis, which reveals the relationship of each statement item to a specified base. When common-size balance sheets are prepared total assets is the base, which is the 100% figure. Every other item on the financial statement is reported as a percentage of that base.

$$\text{Common-size \%} = \frac{\text{Each balance sheet item}}{\text{Total assets}}$$

To calculate the common-size percentage for cell B33, reference the current asset amount in cell B8 and divide by total assets of the same year in cell B11. The resulting cell formula is "=+B8/B11".

5. In column B, prepare formulas that reference the above balance sheet amounts in cells A5..E24 to create the common-size statements. In cells labeled "Sum," create a formula that adds the amounts directly above. Copy formulas to the other three columns.

6. Save and print a copy for your files.

7. Review the common-size statements. What do the percentages for property, plant, and equipment, net, total liabilities, and total stockholders' equity reveal?

Activity 88   **PREPARING TREND PERCENTAGES FOR THE BALANCE SHEETS**

Purpose: · Use an Excel spreadsheet to prepare trend percentages for comparative balance sheets.
                · Understand and interpret amounts reported on trend percentage balance sheets.

1.   Complete Activity 86. Open the Excel file "I&A Ch8" that was created in Activity 86.
2.   Copy the balance sheets created in Activity 86 (cells A5..E24) to a new location starting with cell A55.
3.   Highlight B58..E74 for formatting. Select Format, Cells, and Number. Make the following selections: "Category:" choose Percentage, "Decimal Places:" choose 0. Then click *OK*. Results will not make any sense, but that will be corrected as we continue.

	A	B	C	D	E
55	**FUJI PHOTO FILM Co., LTD**	**TREND**	**PERCENTAGES**		
56					**BASE YEAR**
57	**ASSETS**	**3/31/02**	**3/31/01**	**3/31/00**	**3/31/99**
58	Current assets	Formula	Formula	Formula	Formula
59	Property, plant, and equipment, net	Copy	Copy	Copy	Copy
60	Other assets	Copy	Copy	Copy	Copy
61	TOTAL ASSETS	Copy	Copy	Copy	Copy
62					
63	**LIABILITIES**				
64	Current liabilities	Copy	Copy	Copy	Copy
65	Long-term liabilities	Copy	Copy	Copy	Copy
66	Total liabilities	Copy	Copy	Copy	Copy
67					
68	**STOCKHOLDERS' EQUITY**				
69	Common stock	Copy	Copy	Copy	Copy
70	Retained earnings	Copy	Copy	Copy	Copy
71	Other stockholders' equity	Copy	Copy	Copy	Copy
72	Total stockholders' equity	Copy	Copy	Copy	Copy
73					
74	TOTAL L AND SE	Copy	Copy	Copy	Copy

4.   Trend percentages are a form of horizontal analysis, which studies the percentage change in comparative statements. Trend percentages are 100% for the base year. Amounts reported for other years are expressed as a percentage of the base year amount. To compute trend percentages, divide each item for a following year by the corresponding amount for the base year.

$$\text{Trend \%} = \frac{\underline{\text{Any year \$}}}{\text{Base year \$}}$$

To calculate the trend percentage for cell B58, reference the current asset amount in cell B8 and divide by current assets of the base year in cell E8. The resulting the cell formula is "=+B8/E8".

5.   Prepare formulas in Row 58 that reference the above balance sheet amounts in cells B8..E24 to create the trend percentages. Copy formulas to the other rows.
6.   Create a footer by selecting View, Header and Footer, and Custom Footer. In the "Left section:" enter your name and in the "Right section:" enter Balance Sheet. Save and print a copy for your files.
7.   Compare the trend percentages for total assets to the trend percentages for other accounts. What percentages appear significant? Why?

Activity 89   **CALCULATING RATIOS USING BALANCE SHEET AMOUNTS**

Purpose: · Use an Excel spreadsheet to prepare ratios using amounts from the balance sheet.
                  · Understand and interpret ratio amounts.

1.   Complete Activity 86. Open the Excel file "I&A Ch8" that was created in Activity 86.
2.   Continue formatting as follows:

	A	B	C	D	E
80	**FUJI PHOTO FILM Co., LTD**	**RATIOS**			
81					
82		**3/31/02**	**3/31/01**	**3/31/00**	**3/31/99**
83	CURRENT RATIO	Formula	Formula	Formula	Formula
84	DEBT RATIO	Formula	Formula	Formula	Formula

3.   Highlight B83..E84 for formatting. Select Format, Cells, and Number. Make the following selections: "Category:" choose Number, "Decimal Places:" choose 2. Then click *OK*.

4.   Ratios express the relationship of one number to the other.
      a.   The Current Ratio measures the ability to pay current liabilities with current assets. In general, a (**lower / higher**) ratio indicates a stronger financial position. Risk Management Association reports that the average current ratio for most industries is approximately (**1.50 / 3.50 / 5.50**).

Current ratio =   Current assets
Current liabilities

      b.   The Debt Ratio indicates the proportion of assets financed with debt. In general, a (**lower / higher**) ratio indicates fewer interest and principal obligations. On new borrowing, creditors generally charge (**lower / higher**) interest rates to companies with a low debt ratio. Risk Management Association reports that the average debt ratio for most industries is within the range (**0.37 to 0.47 / 0.57 to 0.67 / 0.87 to 0.97**).

Debt ratio =   Total liabilities
Total assets

5.   Prepare formulas to calculate the current ratio and the debt ratio by referencing the above balance sheet amounts in cells B8..E24.

6.   Save and print a copy for your files.

7.   Review the ratios and discuss what each ratio reveals.

Activity 90   **PREPARING EXCEL GRAPHS**

Purpose: · Use an Excel spreadsheet to prepare graphs using amounts reported on the balance sheet.
                  · Understand and interpret ratio amounts.

1.   Complete Activity 86. Open the Excel file "I&A Ch8" that was created in Activity 86.
2.   Continue formatting as follows:

	A	B	C	D	E
80	**FUJI PHOTO FILM Co., LTD**	**RATIOS**			
81					
82		**3/31/02**	**3/31/01**	**3/31/00**	**3/31/99**
83	CURRENT RATIO	Formula	Formula	Formula	Formula
84	DEBT RATIO	Formula	Formula	Formula	Formula
85					
86		**3/31/02**	**3/31/01**	**3/31/00**	**3/31/99**
87	Total assets	Formula	Formula	Formula	Formula
88	Total liabilities	Formula	Formula	Formula	Formula
89	Total stockholders' equity	Formula	Formula	Formula	Formula

3.   Highlight B87..E89 for formatting. Select Format, Cells, and Number. Make the following selections: "Category:" choose Number, "Decimal Places:" choose 0, "Negative numbers:" choose (1,234). Then click *OK*.

4.   Prepare formulas for rows 87 through 89 that reference the above balance sheet amounts in cells B8..E24.

5.   Create a graph of the current ratio and debt ratio amounts.
      a.   Select Insert, Chart. Use the Chart Wizard.
      b.   "Step 1 of 4" use the Standard Types Column chart and the default Chart sub-type. Click on *Next>*.
      c.   "Step 2 of 4" select the Data Range B82..E84, Series in Rows, and then click on *Next>*.
      d.   "Step 3 of 4" make the chart title "Ratios" and then click on *Next>*.
      e.   "Step 4 of 4" select to make the graph "As new sheet" and then click on *Finish*.
      f.   Graphs visually express relationships. What relationships do you observe?

6.   Create a graph using balance sheet amounts.
      a.   Select Insert, Chart. Use the Chart Wizard.
      b.   "Step 1 of 4" use the Standard Types Column chart and the default Chart sub-type. Click on *Next>*.
      c.   "Step 2 of 4" select the Data Range B86..E89, Series in Rows, and then click on *Next>*.
      d.   "Step 3 of 4" make the chart title "Balance Sheet" and title the Value (Y) axis "$ in millions" and then click on *Next>*.
      e.   "Step 4 of 4" select to make the graph "As new sheet" and then click on *Finish*.
      f.   In the finished graph, the dates appear in the (**same / opposite**) direction of a time line.
      g.   Run your curser over the first bar for 1999. What information is revealed?

7.   Save and print a copy of each graph for your files.

Activity 91 **USING EXCEL GRAPHS IN POWERPOINT**

Purpose: · Use Excel graphs within a PowerPoint slide presentation.

1. Complete Activity 86 and Activity 90.

2. Open PowerPoint. Create a new presentation using a "Blank presentation." Click on *OK*.

3. Create a slide that contains the ratio graph of Fuji Photo Film Co., Ltd. created in Activity 90.
   a. For "Choose an AutoLayout:" select the bar-graph layout and click on *OK*.
   b. Click on "Click to add title" and type in "FUJI PHOTO FILM CO., LTD."
   c. Double click on "Double click to add chart." Select Edit, Import File... (by the bar-graph icon). Open the Excel file created in Activity 90 named "I&A Ch8." Select the worksheet containing the ratio graph. Click on *OK*. To close this box, click outside the graph area of the slide.

4. Create another slide that contains the graph of the balance sheet amounts of Fuji Photo Film Co., Ltd. created in Activity 90.
   a. Select Insert, New Slide. For "Choose an AutoLayout:" select the bar-graph layout and click on *OK*.
   b. Click on "Click to add title" and type in "FUJI PHOTO FILM CO., LTD."
   c. Double click on "Double click to add chart." Select Edit, Import File... (by the bar-graph icon). Open the Excel file created in Activity 90 named "I&A Ch8." Select the worksheet containing the balance sheet graph. Click on *OK*. To close this box, click outside the graph area of the slide.

5. View the slide show.
   a. Select Slide Show, View Show.
   b. Left click to advance to the next slide. View the entire slide show.

6. Print a copy of the slides in handout format for your files.
   a. Select File, Print.
   b. "Print what:" select Handouts. "Slides per page:" select 6. Select "Gray scale" and "Frame slides." Click *OK*.

7. Save your PowerPoint file and name it "I&A Ch8."

Activity 92   **PREPARING MULTI-STEP INCOME STATEMENTS**

Purpose: · Use an Excel spreadsheet to prepare multi-step income statements.
                      · Understand and interpret amounts reported on the income statement.

1. Open an Excel file and name it "I&A Ch8" (if you haven't done so already). Open the second
    worksheet and title it "Income Statement." Enter your name in cell A1, today's date in cell A2,
    and your instructor's name and course in cell A3. Then format as follows:

	A	B	C	D	E
5	**FUJI PHOTO FILM Co., LTD**	**INCOME**	**STATEMENTS**		
6					
7	**12 Months Ending** ($ in millions):	**3/31/02**	**3/31/01**	**3/31/00**	**3/31/99**
8	Revenues	20,046	11,549	11,261	12,004
9	Cost of goods sold	11,698	6,708	6,468	6,512
10	Gross margin	*Formula 1*	*Formula 1*	*Formula 1*	*Formula 1*
11					
12	Operating expenses	*Formula 2*	*Formula 2*	*Formula 2*	*Formula 2*
13	Income from operations	1,408	1,250	1,235	1,380
14					
15	Other gains and losses	*Formula 3*	*Formula 3*	*Formula 3*	*Formula 3*
16	Income before income tax	1,332	1,667	1,147	1,145
17					
18	Income tax expense	592	722	523	580
19	Income before nonrecurring items	*Formula 4*	*Formula 4*	*Formula 4*	*Formula 4*
20					
21	Nonrecurring items/Minority items	*Formula 5*	*Formula 5*	*Formula 5*	*Formula 5*
22	NET INCOME	679	984	709	624

2. In column B, prepare formulas in the order designated. Copy formulas to the other three columns.

3. Highlight B8..E22 for formatting. Select Format, Cells, and Number. Make the following selections:
    "Category:" choose Number, "Decimal Places:" choose 0, "Negative numbers:" choose (1,234).
    Then click *OK*.

4. Save and print a copy for your files.

5. Review the amounts reported on the income statements.
    a. During the fiscal year ending (**3-31-02** / **3-31-01** / **3-31-00**), revenue increased by a
        significant $8.5 billion.

    b. What do the amounts reported for revenues and net income indicate?

Activity 93   **PREPARING COMMON-SIZE INCOME STATEMENTS**

Purpose: · Use an Excel spreadsheet to prepare common-size income statements.
              · Understand and interpret amounts reported on common-size income statements.

1.   Complete Activity 92. Open the Excel file created in Activity 92 titled "I&A Ch8." Open the second worksheet titled "Income Statement."
2.   Copy the income statements created in Activity 92 (cells A5..E22) to a new location starting with cell A30.
3.   Highlight B33..E47 for formatting. Select Format, Cells, and Number. For "Category:" choose Percentage and for "Decimal Places:" choose 1. Then click *OK*. Results will not make any sense, but that will be corrected as we continue.

	A	B	C	D	E
30	**FUJI PHOTO FILM Co., LTD**	**COMMON-SIZE**	**INCOME**	**STATEMENTS**	
31					
32	**12 Months Ending** ($ in millions):	**3/31/02**	**3/31/01**	**3/31/00**	**3/31/99**
33	Revenues	Formula	Copy	Copy	Copy
34	Cost of goods sold	Formula	Copy	Copy	Copy
35	Gross margin	Formula	Copy	Copy	Copy
36					
37	Operating expenses	Formula	Copy	Copy	Copy
38	Income from operations	Formula	Copy	Copy	Copy
39					
40	Other gains and losses	Formula	Copy	Copy	Copy
41	Income before income tax	Formula	Copy	Copy	Copy
42					
43	Income tax expense	Formula	Copy	Copy	Copy
44	Income before nonrecurring items	Formula	Copy	Copy	Copy
45					
46	Nonrecurring items/Minority items	Formula	Copy	Copy	Copy
47	NET INCOME	Formula	Copy	Copy	Copy

4.   Common-size statements are a form of vertical analysis, which reveals the relationship of each statement item to a specified base. When common-size income statements are prepared revenues is the base, which is the 100% figure. Every other item on the financial statement is reported as a percentage of that base.

Common-size % =   <u>Each income statement item</u>
Revenues

To calculate the common-size percentage for cell B33, reference the revenue amount in cell B8 and divide by revenues for the same year in cell B8. The resulting cell formula is "=+B8/B8".

5.   In column B, prepare formulas that reference the above income statement amounts to create the common-size statements. Copy formulas to the other three columns.
6.   Save and print a copy for your files.
7.   Review the common-size statements. What do the common-size percentages reveal?

Activity 94　　PREPARING TREND PERCENTAGES FOR INCOME STATEMENTS

Purpose:　　· Use an Excel spreadsheet to prepare trend percentages for comparative income statements.
　　　　· Understand and interpret amounts reported on trend percentage income statements.

1. Complete Activity 92. Open the Excel file created in Activity 92 titled "I&A Ch8." Open the second worksheet titled "Income Statement."
2. Copy the income statements created in Activity 92 (cells A5..E22) to a new location starting with cell A55.
3. Highlight B58..E72 for formatting. Select Format, Cells, and Number. Make the following selections: "Category:" choose Percentage, "Decimal Places:" choose 0. Then click *OK*. Results will not make any sense, but that will be corrected as we continue.

	A	B	C	D	E
55	**FUJI PHOTO FILM Co., LTD**	**TREND PERCENTAGES**			
56					**BASE YEAR**
57	**12 Months Ending** ($ in millions):	**3/31/02**	**3/31/01**	**3/31/00**	**3/31/99**
58	Revenues	Formula	Formula	Formula	Formula
59	Cost of goods sold	Copy	Copy	Copy	Copy
60	Gross margin	Copy	Copy	Copy	Copy
61					
62	Operating expenses	Copy	Copy	Copy	Copy
63	Income from operations	Copy	Copy	Copy	Copy
64					
65	Other gains and losses	Copy	Copy	Copy	Copy
66	Income before income tax	Copy	Copy	Copy	Copy
67					
68	Income tax expense	Copy	Copy	Copy	Copy
69	Income before nonrecurring items	Copy	Copy	Copy	Copy
70					
71	Nonrecurring items/Minority items	Copy	Copy	Copy	Copy
72	NET INCOME	Copy	Copy	Copy	Copy

4. Trend percentages are a form of horizontal analysis, which studies the percentage change in comparative statements. Trend percentages are 100% for the base year. Amounts reported for other years are expressed as a percentage of the base year amount. To compute trend percentages, divide each item for a following year by the corresponding amount for the base year.

$$\text{Trend \% } = \frac{\textbf{Any year \$}}{\textbf{Base year \$}}$$

To calculate the trend percentage for cell B58, reference the revenue amount in cell B8 and divide by revenue of the base year in cell E8. The resulting cell formula is "=+B8/E8".

5. Prepare formulas in Row 58 that reference the above income statement amounts in cells B8..E22 to create the trend percentages. Copy formulas to the other rows.
6. Create a footer by selecting View, Header and Footer, and Custom Footer. In the "Left section:" enter your name and in the "Right section:" enter Income Statement. Save and print a copy for your files.
7. Compare the trend percentages for revenues to the trend percentages for other accounts. What percentages appear significant? Why?

Activity 95   **CALCULATING PROFITABILITY RATIOS**

Purpose: · Use an Excel spreadsheet to prepare profitability ratios using amounts from the
                    income statement and the balance sheet.
                 · Understand and interpret ratio amounts.

1.   Complete Activity 92. Open the Excel file created in Activity 92 titled "I&A Ch8." Open the
      second worksheet titled "Income Statement." Then format as follows:

	A	B	C	D	E
80	**FUJI PHOTO FILM Co., LTD**	**RATIOS**			
81					
82		**3/31/02**	**3/31/01**	**3/31/00**	**3/31/99**
83	Total assets	24,598	23,629	18,667	17,695
84	Average total assets	Formula	Formula	Formula	
85					
86	Total stockholders' equity	14,177	13,565	13,150	12,127
87	Average stockholders' equity	Formula	Formula	Formula	
88					
89	Interest expense	97	93	83	
90					
91	ASSET TURNOVER	Formula	Formula	Formula	
92					
93	RETURN ON SALES	Formula	Formula	Formula	
94					
95	RETURN ON ASSETS	Formula	Formula	Formula	
96					
97	RETURN ON EQUITY	Formula	Formula	Formula	

2.   a.   Highlight B83..E89 for formatting. Select Format, Cells, and Number. Make the following
            selections: "Category:" choose Number, "Decimal Places:" choose 0. Then click *OK*.
      b.   Highlight B91..E97 for formatting. Select Format, Cells, and Number. Make the following
            selections: "Category:" choose Number, "Decimal Places:" choose 4. Then click *OK*.

3.   Prepare formulas to calculate average total assets and average stockholders' equity by referencing
      the balance sheet amounts immediately above.
                    Average amount =   (Beginning amount + Ending amount)
                                                                2

4.   Ratios express the relationship of one number to the other.
      a.   The Asset Turnover ratio is a measure of efficiency showing the amount of sales produced
            for a given level of assets. It is best when a company can produce (**high / low**) sales with a
            (**high / low**) investment in assets.
                          Asset turnover =   Revenues
                                           Average total assets

      b.   The Return-on-Sales ratio is a measure of profitability showing the percentage of each sales
            dollar earned as net income. A higher rate of return indicates that a (**greater / lesser**)
            proportion of each sales dollar provides net income, while a (**greater / lesser**) proportion is
            absorbed by expenses. The Return-on-Sales ratio varies widely by industry.
                          Return on sales =   Net income
                                           Net sales revenue

c.   The Return-on-Assets ratio is a measure of profitability showing success at using assets to earn net income. A (**high** / **low**) rate of return is preferred. For most companies, (**0.03** / **0.10** / **0.30**) is considered a strong return-on-assets ratio. However, this ratio can vary widely by industry.

$$\text{Return on assets} = \frac{\text{Net income} + \text{Interest expense}}{\text{Average total assets}}$$

d.   The Return-on-Equity ratio is a measure of profitability showing the relationship between net income available to common shareholders and the amounts invested by common shareholders. The higher the rate of return, the (**more** / **less**) successful the company. For most companies, (**0.05** / **0.15** / **0.50**) is considered a strong return-on-equity ratio.

$$\text{Return on equity} = \frac{\text{Net income} - \text{Preferred dividends}}{\text{Average common stockholders' equity}}$$

5.   Prepare formulas to calculate asset turnover, return on sales, return on assets, and return on equity by referencing income statement amounts in cells B5..E24 and balance sheet amounts in cells B83..E87. Use the above formulas.

6.   Save and print a copy for your files.

7.   For the most recent year, the return-on-assets ratio is _____ while the return-on-equity ratio is _____. Borrowing at a lower rate than the company's return on equity is called using leverage. Leverage is being used when the return-on-asset ratio is (**greater** / **less**) than the return-on-equity ratio. This company (**is** / **is not**) using leverage.

8.   Review the ratios and discuss what each ratio reveals.

a.   Asset turnover

b.   Return on sales

c.   Return on assets

d.   Return on equity

Activity 96   **COMPARATIVE ANALYSIS**

Purpose: · Use an Excel spreadsheet to compare two companies.
                  · Analyze amounts reported on the income statement and profitability ratios.

1.   Complete Activities 92, 93 ,94, and 95.
2.   Open the Excel file created in Activity 92 titled "I&A Ch8." Open the second worksheet titled "Income Statement."
3.   To copy this worksheet. Select Edit, Move or Copy Sheet…, (move to end), select Create a copy. Then click *OK*.
4.   Title this new worksheet "Kodak." Enter your name in cell A1, today's date in cell A2, and your instructor's name and course in cell A3.
5.   Change references from Fuji to Eastman Kodak Company. Change dates and amounts as follows:

	A	B	C	D	E
5	**EASTMAN KODAK Co.**				
6					
7		**12/31/02**	**12/31/01**	**12/31/00**	**12/31/99**
8	Revenues	12,835	13,229	13,994	14,089
9	Cost of goods sold	8,225	8,661	8,375	8,086
10					
11					
12					
13	Income from operations	1,220	352	2,214	1,990
14					
15					
16	Income before income tax	946	115	2,132	2,109
17					
18	Income tax expense	153	34	725	717
19					
20					
21					
22	NET INCOME	770	76	1,407	1,392

	A	B	C	D	E
80	**EASTMAN KODAK Co.**				
81					
82		**12/31/02**	**12/31/01**	**12/31/00**	**12/31/99**
83	Total assets	13,369	13,362	14,212	14,370
84					
85					
86	Total stockholders' equity	2,777	2,894	3,428	3,912
87					
88					
89	Interest expense	173	219	178	

6.   Formulas will automatically adjust to the new information.

7.   Create a footer by selecting View, Header and Footer, and Custom Footer. In the "Left section:" enter your name and in the "Right section:" enter Eastman Kodak. Save and print a copy for your files.

8. Review the information for Eastman Kodak Company.
   a. After reviewing the income statement amounts, (**1999 / 2000 / 2001 / 2002**) appears to be the worst year for Eastman Kodak Company. Why?

   b. Review the common-size income statements. What additional information supports your response to part (a)?

   c. Review the trend percentages. What additional information supports your response to part (a)?

   d. Review the ratios. What additional information supports your response to part (a)?

   e. Review all of the financial information of Eastman Kodak. What does this information indicate?

9. Open the worksheet titled "Income Statement" and print a copy (if you haven't done so already). Compare the income statement information of Eastman Kodak with the income statement information of Fuji Photo Film Co., Ltd. What does this comparison reveal?

Activity 97   **PREPARING STATEMENTS OF CASH FLOW**

Purpose: · Use an Excel spreadsheet to prepare statements of cash flow.
               · Understand and interpret amounts reported on trend percentage statements of cash flow.

1.   Open an Excel file and name it "I&A Ch8" (if you haven't done so already). Open the third worksheet and title it "Cash Flow." Enter your name in cell A1, today's date in cell A2, and your instructor's name and course in cell A3. Then format as follows:

	A	B	C	D	E
5	**FUJI PHOTO FILM Co., LTD**	**STATEMENTS OF CASH FLOW**			
6					
7	**12 Months Ending ($ in millions):**	**3/31/02**	**3/31/01**	**3/31/00**	**3/31/99**
8	**Cash from operating activities**	2,060	1,169	1,773	1,312
9					
10	Capital expenditures	(1,326)	(896)	(753)	(996)
11	Other investing cash flow items	*Formula 1*	*Formula 1*	*Formula 1*	*Formula 1*
12	**Cash from investing activities**	(2,461)	(2,169)	(901)	(1,161)
13					
14	Cash dividends paid	(102)	(97)	(97)	(97)
15	Issuance (Retirement) of stock, net	(4)	(1)	-0-	-0-
16	Issuance (Retirement) of debt, net	*Formula 2*	*Formula 2*	*Formula 2*	*Formula 2*
17	**Cash from financing activities**	(371)	(624)	(208)	(234)
18					
19	Foreign exchange effects	67	33	(45)	(38)
20	**Net change in cash**	*Formula 3*	*Formula 3*	*Formula 3*	*Formula 3*
21	+ Beginning cash & equivalents	*Formula 4*	*Formula 4*	*Formula 4*	4,985
22	= Ending cash & equivalents	*Formula 5*	*Formula 5*	*Formula 5*	*Formula 5*

2.   In column B, prepare formulas in the order designated. Copy formulas to the other three columns.

3.   a.   Highlight B8..E22 for formatting. Select Format, Cells, and Number. Make the following selections: "Category:" choose Number, "Decimal Places:" choose 0, "Negative numbers:" choose (1,234). Then click *OK*.

4.   Save and print a copy for your files.

5.   Review the statements of cash flow. What do the amounts indicate for cash from operating activities? Cash from investing activities? Cash from financing activities? Net change in cash?

Activity 98   **PREPARING TREND PERCENTAGES**
                            FOR STATEMENTS OF CASH FLOW

Purpose: · Use an Excel spreadsheet to prepare trend percentages for comparative income
                  statements.
                · Understand and interpret amounts reported on trend percentage income statements.

1.   Complete Activity 97. Open the Excel file created in Activity 97 titled "I&A Ch8." Open the third
     worksheet titled "Cash Flow."
2.   Copy the statements of cash flow created in Activity 97 (cells A5..E22) to a new location starting
     with cell A30.
3.   Highlight B33..E47 for formatting. Select Format, Cells, and Number. Make the following
     selections: "Category:" choose Percentage, "Decimal Places:" choose 0. Then click *OK*. Results
     will not make any sense, but that will be corrected as we continue.

	A	B	C	D	E
30	**FUJI PHOTO FILM Co., LTD**	**TREND**	**PERCENTAGES**		
31					**BASE YEAR**
32	**12 Months Ending** ($ in millions):	**3/31/02**	**3/31/01**	**3/31/00**	**3/31/99**
33	**Cash from operating activities**	Formula	Formula	Formula	Formula
34					
35	Capital expenditures	Copy	Copy	Copy	Copy
36	Other investing cash flow items	Copy	Copy	Copy	Copy
37	**Cash from investing activities**	Copy	Copy	Copy	Copy
38					
39	Cash dividends paid	Copy	Copy	Copy	Copy
40	Issuance (Retirement) of stock, net	Copy	Copy	Copy	Copy
41	Issuance (Retirement) of debt, net	Copy	Copy	Copy	Copy
42	**Cash from financing activities**	Copy	Copy	Copy	Copy
43					
44	Foreign exchange effects	Copy	Copy	Copy	Copy
45	**Net change in cash**	Copy	Copy	Copy	Copy
46	+ Beginning cash & equivalents	Copy	Copy	Copy	Copy
47	= Ending cash & equivalents	Copy	Copy	Copy	Copy

4.   Trend percentages are a form of horizontal analysis, which studies the percentage change in
     comparative statements. Trend percentages are 100% for the base year. Amounts reported for other
     years are expressed as a percentage of the base year amount. To compute trend percentages, divide
     each item for a following year by the corresponding amount for the base year.

$$\text{Trend \%} = \frac{\text{Any year \$}}{\text{Base year \$}}$$

To calculate the trend percentage for cell B33, reference the cash from operating activities amount
in cell B8 and divide by cash from operating activities of the base year in cell E8. The resulting cell
formula is "=+B8/E8".

5.   Prepare formulas in Row 33 that reference the above statements of cash flow amounts in cells
     B8..E22 to create the trend percentages. Copy formulas to the other rows.
6.   Save and print a copy for your files.
7.   Review the trend percentages. What percentages appear significant? Why?

Activity 99   **COMPREHENSIVE ANALYSIS**

Purpose: · Analyze amounts reported on the financial statements.

1.   Complete Activities 86-89 for the balance sheet, Activities 92-95 for the income statement, and
      Activities 97-98 for the statement of cash flows.
2.   Open the Excel file titled "I&A Ch8."
3.   Print the following worksheets (if you haven't already done so): Balance Sheet, Income Statement,
      and Cash Flows.
4.   Review the amounts on the three financial statements.
      a.   Did the amounts invested in property, plant, and equipment – income-producing assets –
            actually result in increased revenues? Increased cash flows?

            How did the company finance their asset purchases? How can you tell?

      b.   Review the common-size income statements. What additional information supports your
            response to part (a)?

      c.   Review the trend percentages. What additional information supports your response to part
            (a)?

      d.   Review the ratios. What additional information supports your response to part (a)?

      e.   Review all of the financial information of Fuji Photo Film Co., Ltd. What does this
            information indicate?

CHAPTER 9

INTERNET RESEARCH

PURPOSE: Chapter 9 introduces Internet research and those websites that are most helpful in locating financial information. This series of activities lead the students through the research process by identifying a company's Web address, ticker symbol, and SIC code, defining competitors, finding financial statements and industry ratios, and exploring general information available about a particular company. These activities prepare the student for the research required to complete the capstone project in Chapter 10.

QUESTION: Does Coca-Cola report more domestic or international sales? Read this chapter to find the answer.

FEATURED CORPORATIONS

AMR Corporation (AMR NYSE) owns American Airlines and American Eagle. American Airlines is the United States' largest air carrier with a fleet of more than 800 jets serving approximately 160 destinations in the Americas, Europe, and the Pacific Rim (some through code-sharing). The carrier has recently expanded by acquiring TWA. In the airline industry slowdown that has followed September 11, 2001, American Airlines is working to reduce its capacity, its fleet, and its workforce. www.amrcorp.com

Anheuser-Busch Companies, Inc. (BUD NYSE) is the world's largest brewer and the largest beer producer in the United States with approximately half of the market share. It makes Budweiser, the nation's top-ranked beer, along with Bud Light, Michelob, and Busch. It is the largest recycler of aluminum cans in the world and one of the largest manufacturers of aluminum cans in the United States. It also operates amusement parks such as Busch Gardens and Sea World. www.anheuser-busch.com

Berkshire Hathaway Inc. (BRK NYSE) is where billionaire Warren Buffett, one of the world's richest men, pools his investments. It operates in the insurance industry and uses the "float," the cash collected before insurance claims are paid out, to invest in a portfolio of businesses. Buffett and his wife Susan own about 40% of the company. www.berkshirehathaway.com

Coca-Cola Company, The (KO NYSE) was established in 1886 and is now the world's largest soft drink company operating in approximately 200 countries and commanding approximately 50% of the global soft-drink market. The firm, which does no bottling, sells about 300 drink brands, including Coca-Cola, Sprite, Barq's, Minute Maid, and Dasani and Evian water. www.cocacola.com

Ford Motor Company (F NYSE) began a manufacturing revolution in the 1900s with its mass production assembly lines. Now the company is the world's largest pickup truck maker and the #2 producer of vehicles behind General Motors. Vehicles are produced under the names of Ford, Jaguar, Lincoln, Mercury, Volvo, and Aston Martin. Ford has a controlling interest in Mazda and has purchased BMW's Land Rover SUV operations. It also owns the #1 auto finance company, Ford Motor Credit, and Hertz, the world's #1 car-rental firm. The Ford family owns about 40% of the company's voting stock. www.ford.com

Harley-Davidson Corporation (HDI NYSE) is the nation's #1 seller of heavyweight motorcycles and the only major maker of domestic motorcycles. The company offers 24 models of touring and custom Harleys through a worldwide network of more than 1,350 dealers. Harley models include the Electra Glide, the Sportster, and the Fat Boy. The company also makes motorcycles under the Buell nameplate. Besides its bikes, Harley-Davidson sells attitude -- goods licensed with the company name include a line of clothing and accessories. www.harley-davidson.com

Home Depot Inc., The (HD NYSE) is the world's largest home improvement chain and second-largest retailer after Wal-Mart. It owns and operates 1,500 do-it-yourself warehouse retail stores in the United States, Canada, and Latin America. These stores offer building materials, home improvement products, and related furnishings. www.homedepot.com

Intel Corporation (INTC Nasdaq) is the largest producer of semiconductors in the world currently possessing 80% of the market share. Intel's most notable products include its Pentium and Celeron microprocessors. Intel also makes flash memories and is #1 globally in this market. Dell is the company's largest customer. www.intel.com

Panera Bread Company (PNRA Nasdaq) is a leader in the quick-casual breakfast and lunch restaurant business with more than 470 sandwich eateries in about 30 states. Its bakery/cafes, which operate under the Saint Louis Bread Company name as well as its signature brand, offer made-to-order sandwiches using a variety of fresh artisan breads, including Asagio cheese, focaccia, and its classic sourdough bread. Its menu also features soups, salads, and gourmet coffees. In addition, Panera sells its bread, bagels, and pastries to go. CEO Ron Shaich owns more than 25% of the company. www.panerabread.com

Papa John's International (PZZA Nasdaq) is the #3 pizza chain (behind Yum! Brands' Pizza Hut division and Domino's) with about 3,000 pizzerias across the U.S. and about a dozen other countries. Its restaurants offer a variety of pizza styles and topping choices, as well as a few specialty pies such as The Works and All the Meats. Papa John's locations typically offer delivery and carryout service only. In addition to its signature brand, the company has 140 Perfect Pizza franchises in the UK. The company has developed a commissary system that supplies pizza dough, food products, and paper products to company-owned and franchised restaurants. www.papajohns.com

Starbucks Corporation (SBUX Nasdaq) is the leading specialty coffee retailer with 5,900 coffee shops positioned throughout 25 countries in office buildings, malls, airports, and other locations. In addition to coffee, Starbucks offers coffee beans, pastries, mugs, coffee makers, coffee grinders, and even coffee ice cream. The company also sells its beans to restaurants, businesses, airlines, and hotels, and it offers mail order and online catalogs. Starbucks has expanded into Frappuccino, a bottled coffee drink, jointly with PepsiCo. www.starbucks.com

Wal-Mart Stores, Inc. (WMT NYSE) is the largest retailer in the world with about 4,600 stores. Its sales are greater than Sears, Target, and Kroger combined. Its stores include Wal-Mart discount stores, Wal-Mart Supercenters that are a combination discount and grocery store, and Sam's Club membership-only warehouse stores. Most Wal-Mart stores are in the United States, but international expansion has made it the #1 retailer in Canada and Mexico. Wal-Mart also has operations in South America, Asia, and Europe. Wal-Mart is rated Number 1 on the 2002 Fortune 500 list. www.walmartstores.com

----

Numerous sources including *Hoover's Company Capsules*, Hoover's, Inc., 2003.

Activity 100   **GATHERING RESEARCH INFORMATION**
Using www.hoovers.com

Purpose: · Use the Internet to help gather information essential to researching a company.

This is a good site to start gathering information about companies: the company's Web address, stock ticker symbol, SIC code, general description, competitors, and financial information.

1.   Research Anheuser-Busch by typing in <u>Anheuser</u> in the "Search by Company Name for" box and clicking on *GO*. Then click on *Capsule* for the Anheuser-Busch Companies, Inc.
   Note: The key icon indicates member information. All other information is provided free to nonmembers.

   a.   What is the company's Web address?   <u>www</u>._____

   b.   What is the company's 3-digit stock symbol? _____
        Note: The 3-digit stock symbol is helpful for stock price quotes and company computer searches.

   c.   On which stock exchange does this company trade? (**New York Stock Exchange / NASDAQ**)

   d.   List the top three competitors.

        _____   _____   _____

2.   Review the written description of the company and briefly summarize the essential information.

3.   Click on the *Financial* tab in the horizontal menu toward the top of the page.
   On the "Free" line of information, click on *Annual Financials*.
   Record the following information for the three years of annual financials provided.

Year ended December (*$ in millions*)	_____	_____	_____
Revenue	$ _____	$ _____	$ _____
Total Net Income	_____	_____	_____
Total Assets	_____	_____	_____
Total Liabilities	_____	_____	_____

   Review the financial information above. What does this financial information indicate?

4. Click on the *News and Analysis* tab in the horizontal menu toward the top of the page. Under "News and Commentary" click on *Current Stories Mentioning Anheuser-Busch*. Read one of the news stories and *summarize* the main points below.

5. Go back to the horizontal menu and click on the *Industry* tab.
    a. What is the primary industry of this company and its corresponding SIC code?
        Note: SIC is an acronym for Standard Industrial Classification Code and is an industry coding system used to report information on U.S. businesses. It is helpful for industry computer searches.

    b. This company participates in what secondary industries?

    c. Under "Primary Industry" click on *Beverages – Brewers* to display other companies within this industry. Approximately how many companies are listed in this industry? _____

    d. Click on *Capsule* for one of the companies listed. Review the information displayed and comment on one item of interest.

6. Explore another feature of this website. *Comment* on what you found and whether you consider this information useful.
    Remember: The key icon indicates member information. All other information is provided free to nonmembers.

7. REVIEW: List at least five items of information provided on this website that would be useful in researching a corporation.

Please note: Internet websites are constantly being updated; therefore, if the information is not found where indicated, please explore the website further to find the information.

**IDENTIFYING FORTUNE 500 COMPANIES AND
RESEARCHING COMPANY INFORMATION**
Using www.fortune.com

Purpose: · Identify Fortune 500, America's Most Admired, and Best to Work For companies.
· Research information about a company.

This website provides lists of companies ranked by Fortune magazine and related company information.

1. In the left-hand column, click on *Fortune 500* companies. Record the five top-ranked companies,
   their reported revenues, and current quote (ticker) symbol.
   (1) _____ $ _____ million   Symbol _____
   (2) _____ $ _____ million   Symbol _____
   (3) _____ $ _____ million   Symbol _____
   (4) _____ $ _____ million   Symbol _____
   (5) _____ $ _____ million   Symbol _____

2. In the left-hand column, click on *America's Most Admired* companies. Record the six top-ranked
   companies and their reported revenues.
   (1) _____   (4) _____
   (2) _____   (5) _____
   (3) _____   (6) _____

3. In the left-hand column, click on *100 Best To Work For* companies.
   Record the top-ranked company: (1) _____

   Click on the company name and record the following information:
   What is the most common entry-level job (professional)? _____
       Entry-level salary? $ _____
   How many hours are spent on professional training?   _____ hours per year

   Why was this company ranked #1?

4. In the left-hand column, click on *50 Best For Minorities* companies.
   Record the top-ranked company: (1) _____

   Click on the company name and record what percent of the workforce is:
   Asian? _____%   Black? _____%   Hispanic? _____%   Native American? _____%

5. In the left-hand column, in the SEARCH FORTUNE box type in any company name ranked above
    to search for news related items. Select one of the articles and summarize the main points below.

Please note: Internet websites are constantly being updated; therefore, if the information is not found where indicated,
please explore the website further to find the information.

Activity 102   **FINDING FOUR YEARS OF FINANCIAL STATEMENT INFORMATION**
AND ANALYZING THE BALANCE SHEET
Using yahoo.multexinvestor.com/

Purpose: · Use the Internet to find four years of comparable financial statement information.
· Understand and interpret amounts reported on the balance sheet.

This is a great website to find and print a five-year set of financial statements.

1.   Find four years of comparable annual balance sheets of Ford Motor Company.
a.   To retrieve the balance sheet, enter **F**, the ticker symbol for Ford Motor Company, in the box labeled " Quick Quote."   Then click on *GO*.
b.   In the menu to the left, click on *Financial Statements* and then click on *Balance Sheet*.
c.   To obtain a printed copy, click on the " *printable*" button for 5 years of comparable financial statements. *Hint*: Be certain you are printing the *annual* rather than the quarterly financials.

2.   Using the financial information for Ford Motor Co., prepare the condensed balance sheet form below.

FORD MOTOR CO. ($ in millions) **Dated:**	(Most recent year)	_____	_____	_____
Current assets	$	$	$	$
Property, plant, and equipment, net				
Other assets				
TOTAL assets	$	$	$	$

Current liabilities	$	$	$	$
Long-term liabilities				
Contributed capital				
Retained earnings				
Treasury stock and other stockholders' equity				
TOTAL liabilities and stockholders' equity	$	$	$	$

Hint: Make certain CA + PPE, net + Other = Total assets and CL + LTL + RE + Other = Total L&SE.

Using the condensed balance sheet information on the previous page, answer the following questions:

3. Total liabilities were \$_____ million for the earliest year reported and \$_____ million for the most recent year reported. Since the earliest year reported, this account has (**increased / decreased**) by \$_____ million, which is a _____% (**increase / decrease**).

   What might explain this change?

4. Retained earnings were \$_____ million for the earliest year reported and \$_____ million for the most recent year reported. Since the earliest year reported, this account has (**increased / decreased**) by \$_____ million, which is a _____% (**increase / decrease**).

   What might explain this change?

5. Compute the **current ratio** for the last two years (Current assets / Current liabilities).
   (Most recent year) _____   _____
   This trend is generally considered (**favorable / unfavorable**).

   Does this company have the ability to pay its current debt? (**Yes / No**) Explain.

6. Compute the **debt ratio** for the last two years (Total liabilities / Total assets).
   (Most recent year) _____   _____
   In general, the direction of this trend indicates that a company is assuming (**more / less**) financial risk. This company is primarily financing assets with (**debt / equity**).

   What might explain this choice of financing?

7. Review the balance sheet and ratio information. This balance sheet indicates a (**strengthening / stable / weakening**) financial position. Support your response with at least two observations.

8. Explore another feature of this website. *Comment* on what you found and whether you consider this information useful.

Please note: Internet websites are constantly being updated; therefore, if the information is not found where indicated, please explore the website further to find the information.

Activity 103   **FINDING FINANCIAL INFORMATION IN EXCEL FORMAT AND ANALYZING THE INCOME STATEMENT**
Using edgarscan.pwcglobal.com/servlets/edgarscan

Purpose: · Use the Internet to view and save financial statement information in Excel format.
· Understand and interpret amounts reported on the income statement.

At this website company financials can be viewed in Excel format and compared with other companies. Play with the right click on graphs to view source information.

1. Find Home Depot financial information by clicking on the "Company Name" scroll bar and selecting *Ticker Symbol*: Then enter the ticker symbol <u>HD</u> in the box and click on *Search*.

2. Click on (*business*). Review the information presented and then answer the following questions.

    At the end of the most recent year, Home Depot was operating how many stores? _____ stores
    A typical Home Depot store stocks approximately _____ to _____ product items, including variations in color and size.

    Summarize Home Depot's OPERATING STRATEGY.

    At the end of the most recent year, what percentage of sales was earned by each of the following Product Groups?
    Building materials, lumber, and millwork   _____%
    Plumbing, electrical, and kitchen   _____%
    Hardware and seasonal   _____%
    Paint, flooring, and wall coverings   _____%

3. Go back to the main page and click on (*Retail-Lumber and Other Building Materials Dealers*). Use the scroll bar to select *Net Income*.

    Record the following information for the three highest ranked companies:

Company	Net Income	Rank
_____	$_____	#1
_____	$_____	#2
_____	$_____	#3

4. Go back to the main page and click on *Benchmarking Assistant*.
    a. Use the "All" scroll bar to select *Income*. Click on *Next* six more times viewing graphs of income statement information. Comment on your observations and what they might indicate.

b. Double click on the vertical bar representing net income for the most recent year of information. Which financial statement appears?

_____

For the three most recent years presented, record the following financial information:
Fiscal year ended: _____   _____   _____

NET SALES $_____ million $_____ million $_____ million
NET EARNINGS $_____ million $_____ million $_____ million

5. Go back to the main page and scroll down until you find " Annual Filings (10-K's by Filing Period):" and click on the *most recent 10-K information*.

Scroll down to the " Income Statement" and then click on *Excel Spreadsheet*.
Note: If you choose, this Excel spreadsheet may be saved to your computer.

a. Record the financial information requested in the chart below.

($ in millions) **Fiscal year ended:**	_____ (Most recent year)	_____	_____
Net sales	$	$	$
Cost of goods sold			
Gross margin			
Operating expenses			
Income from operations			
Other gains and losses			
Income before income tax			
Income tax expense			
Net income	$	$	$

b. Review the above information. *Comment* on your observations and what they might indicate.

6. What are three ways this website presents financial information for analysis?

7. Can you figure out how to compare graph information of two different companies using the *Benchmarking Assistant*? (**Yes / No**)

Please note: Internet websites are constantly being updated; therefore, if the information is not found where indicated, please explore the website further to find the information.

Activity 104   **USING A COMPANY ANNUAL REPORT**
AND ANALYZING THE STATEMENT OF CASH FLOWS
Using www.cocacola.com

Purpose: · Use annual report information to research a company.
              · Understand and interpret amounts reported on the statement of cash flows.

This company website contains a wealth of corporate and investor information.

1.   Watch the introduction and then select "The Coca-Cola Company."

2.   Under "Investor" select "Financials" and then *Annual Reports*. Locate *the most recent annual report*.
    a.   Review the *Financial Highlights*.
          For the most recent year, record the "Unit case sales (in billions)" for the following classifications:

                International operations   _____ billion unit case sales
                North American operations   _____ billion unit case sales
                Worldwide   _____ billion unit case sales

          Review the above unit case sales information. What do these figures indicate?

    b.   Review the *Letter to Share Owners*.
          Briefly summarize the main points of the letter.

          Who is the letter from?

    c.   Review the *Operations Review*.

          How does Coca-Cola measure growth?

          On which continent does Coca-Cola generate the greatest sales volume?

    d.   Explore other information provided by the annual report and summarize one item that you found of particular interest.

    e.   A company website and the annual report are a (**valuable / worthless**) source of company and investor information.

f. Review the *Financial Section* of the Annual Report and find the information provided by the Statement of Cash Flows in the "Liquidity and Capital Resources" section.

1. Summarize the cash flow information by preparing the form below.

Fiscal year ended: ($ in millions)	———————— (most recent year)	————————	————————
Net cash inflows (outflows) from **operating activities**	$	$	$
Net cash inflows (outflows) from **investing activities**			
Net cash inflows (outflows) from **financing activities**			

2. Evaluate the cash flow information by answering the questions below.

a. The primary source of cash is (**operating / investing / financing**) activities, which typically indicates a (**strong / weak**) cash position.

b. The company is (**purchasing / selling**) more property, plant, and equipment and investments, which typically indicates a(n) (**expanding / contracting**) business.

c. The company is (**borrowing / repaying**) debt, (**purchasing / issuing**) stock, and (**paying / not paying**) dividends.

d. Overall, The Coca-Cola Company reports a (**strong / weak**) cash position. *Support* your response with at least two observations.

Please note: Internet websites are constantly being updated; therefore, if the information is not found where indicated, please explore the website further to find the information.

Activity 105 **FINDING AND ANALYZING COMPANY AND INDUSTRY RATIOS**

Using moneycentral.msn.com

Purpose: · Use the Internet to find company and industry ratio information.
             · Understand and interpret information reported by company and industry ratios.

This website provides key company and industry ratio information along with market and financial information.

1.   On the screen, _____ points are reported for the Dow (Jones Industrial Average).

2.   Retrieve market information by typing <u>HDI</u> in the "Get Quote:" box and then clicking on *Go*. The information displayed is for the _____ Corporation.
     In the chart on the next page, record the company information for:
     a.   Earnings/Share
     b.   Current dividend yield

3.   Financial publications refer to ratios using different titles. The ratio titles used in this text are listed on the left and those used on this website on the right. Identify the titles referring to the same ratio by placing the letter next to the appropriate title.

     a.   Acid-test ratio   _____ Interest coverage ratio
     b.   Times-interest-earned ratio   _____ Net profit margin ratio
     c.   Return on sales   _____ Quick ratio

4.   In the left-hand column select *Financial Results* and then *Key Ratios*. For each ratio listed below, record the company and industry ratio information in the chart on the next page.

     Select *Financial Condition* and record information for the:
     a.   Current ratio
     b.   Acid-test ratio
     c.   Debt ratio (calculate) = [Debt to Equity ratio / (1 + Debt to Equity ratio)]
     d.   Times-interest-earned ratio
     e.   Book value per share of common share

     Select *Management Efficiency* and record information for the:
     f.   Accounts receivable turnover ratio
     g.   Days' sales in receivables (calculate) = [365 days / Accounts receivable turnover ratio in (f)]
     h.   Inventory turnover ratio

     Select *Profit Margins %* and record information for:
     i.   Return on sales

     Select *Investment Returns %* and record information for:
     j.   Return on assets
     k.   Return on common stockholders' equity

     Select *Price Ratios* and record information for the:
     l.   Price/earnings ratio

Hint: To print all ratio information, click on *Print Report* and select "Key Ratios."

RATIOS	Company Ratios	Industry Norms
1. Current ratio		
2. Acid-test ratio		
3. Accounts receivable turnover		
4. Days' sales in receivables		
5. Inventory turnover		
6. Debt ratio		
7. Times-interest-earned		
8. Return on sales		
9. Return on assets		
10. Return on common stockholders' equity		
11. Earnings per share of common stock		
12. Price/earnings ratio		
13. Dividend yield		
14. Book value per share of common stock		

5. Analyzing the above ratio information.
   a. For each ratio listed above, circle the stronger ratio.

   b. Harley-Davidson has (**stronger / weaker**) short-term liquidity than the industry average. Which ratios provide this information? Why is short-term liquidity important?

   c. Harley-Davidson's accounts receivable turnover is (**more / less**) efficient than the industry average. How can you tell? What does this indicate?

d. Harley-Davidson's inventory turnover is (**more / less**) efficient than the industry average. How can you tell? What does this indicate?

e. Harley-Davidson is primarily financed by (**debt / equity**). Which ratio provides this information? What does this ratio help measure? Do creditors generally prefer a high or low value? Why?

f. Harley-Davidson is (**more / less**) profitable than the industry average. How can you tell? Do these ratios have a short-term or a long-term focus? Where might too much focus on these ratios lead?

g. On the website select *Ten Year Summary*. Review the information provided for Return on Equity and Return on Assets. What additional information is revealed about Harley-Davidson's financial position? Is this information helpful?

h. Review all of the information recorded above. Harley-Davidson (**does / does not**) compare favorably with industry averages. Support your judgment with at least two observations.

6. Explore another feature of this website. *Comment* on what you found and whether you consider this information useful.

- To review specific ratios, refer to Chapter 1: Activities 5, 6, 7, 8, 9, and Chapter 5.
- It is recommended to assign this activity before assigning Activity 112: Part III: Compute Ratios and Compare to Industry Norms.
- *Please note*: Internet websites are constantly being updated; therefore, if the information is not found where indicated, please explore the website further to find the information.

MARKET RESEARCH
Using bigcharts.marketwatch.com

Purpose:
    · Use the Internet to research quotes and historical stock information for specific companies.
    · Use the Internet to research historical information for the Dow Jones Industrial Average.

This website provides research and stock quote information on over 24,000 stocks, mutual funds, and major indexes from 1970 to the present.

1. On the screen, _____ points are reported for the Dow Jones Industrial Average (DJIA).

2. In the "Enter Symbol/Keywords:" box type in SBUX (Starbucks) and then click on *QUICK CHART*. Use the scroll down menu to select "5 years."

   The stock price was Last $_____. The 52 Week Range was $_____ to $_____.

   View the charts. What does the stock quote and information provided by the charts indicate?

3. In the "Enter Symbol/Keywords:" box type in AMR (American Airlines) and click on *QUICK CHART*.
   What does the stock quote and information provided by the charts indicate?

4. In the "Enter Symbol/Keywords:" box type in BRKA (Berkshire Hathaway) and click on *QUICK CHART*.
   What does the stock quote and information provided by the charts indicate?

5. In the "Enter Symbol/Keywords:" box type in INTC (Intel) and click on *INTERACTIVE CHARTING*.
   Intel's market high of approximately $_____ per share was reported on approximately _____. (date) The stock is now trading at $_____ per share.

   In the left-hand menu, click on "compare to" and in the "Symbol(s):" box that opened type in MSFT (Microsoft). Click on *DRAW CHART*. What does the information provided by the charts indicate?

In the left-hand scroll-down menu under "Index:" select DJIA (Dow Jones Industrial Average). Click on *DRAW CHART*. What does the information provided by the charts indicate?

6. In the "Enter Symbol or Keyword:" box type in <u>DJIA</u> (Dow Jones Industrial Average). Click on <u>Quick Chart</u>.

The DJIA was Last _____ points. The 52 Week Range was _____ points to _____ points.

In the scroll-down menu at the top, change "5 years" to "All Data."

Review the top chart. The DJIA was approximately _____ points in January of 1970, took its first 1,000-point plunge during the year of _____, and peaked during January of the year _____.

What does the information provided by the charts indicate to investors?

7. In the horizontal menu toward the top of the page click on "Historical Quotes."
   Use this screen to answer the following questions:

On November 14, 1972, the DJIA closed for the first time above _____ points.

The DJIA closed at: _____ points on December 31, 1985.
_____ points on December 31, 1990.
_____ points on December 31, 1995.
_____ points on December 31, 2000.

8. In the horizontal menu toward the top of the page, in the "Enter Symbol/Keywords:" box type in <u>DJIA</u>. Click on *JAVA CHART*. In the left-hand menu, under <u>Chart Options</u> change the "1 Year" scroll bar to "*1 Decade*." Use the top chart to discover the following information:

The close on 12/31/2002 was approximately _____ points.

In the left-hand menu, under <u>Chart Options</u> change the "Daily" scroll bar to *Yearly*. Use the top chart to discover the following information:

The DJIA peaked at _____ points during the year _____.

9. Explore another feature of this website. *Comment* on what you found and whether you consider this information useful.

Please note: Internet websites are constantly being updated; therefore, if the information is not found where indicated, please explore the website further to find the information.

FINANCIAL ANALYSIS
Using www.morningstar.com

Purpose: · Use the Internet to find ten years of comparable financial statement information.
· Use the Internet to find ten years of common-size and ratio information.

This website provides stock quote and financial analysis information, including trends over the past ten years.

1. To find the current stock quote for Papa John's International, in the "Use Quicktake Reports:" box type in <u>PZZA</u> and click on *GO*.

   The stock price was Last $_____. The 52 Week Range was $_____ to $_____.

2. In the horizontal menu, under "Snapshot" click on *Company Snapshot*.

   a. What does Papa John's International do?

   b. What does the "Analyst Report Summary" say?

   c. What are the following "Morningstar Stock Grades" for the company?

      Growth _____   Profitability _____   Financial Health _____

      Hint: Click on "Morningstar Stock Grades" to find the information behind the ratings.

   d. At the bottom of the screen click on <u>*View industry peers*</u>.

      How does Papa John's International compare to others in the industry?

3. In the horizontal menu, under "10-Yr Financials" find the following information:

   BALANCE SHEET
   a. Papa John's International appears to be a relatively (**new / old**) company.

   b. What does the trend in total assets indicate?

   c. Using the COMMON-SIZE information.
      What's happened to "Net PP&E" (property, plant, and equipment) as a percentage of total assets? What does this indicate?

   Note: The + icon indicates member information. All other information is available to nonmembers.

d.   Using the EFFICIENCY RATIOS information.
     What's happened to the " Days in Inventory" and the " Inventory Turnover" ratios? What
     might this indicate?

INCOME STATEMENT

a.   What does the trend in revenues indicate?

b.   Using the COMMON-SIZE information. What's happened to the " EBT (earnings before tax)
     Margin" ? What does this indicate?

c.   Using the GROWTH information. What's happened to revenue growth? What might this
     indicate?

STATEMENT OF CASH FLOWS

a.   What's happened to " Cash from Operations" ? What does this indicate?

b.   What's happened to " Cap Ex" (capital expenditures)? What does this indicate?

c.   Does this company pay dividends? (**Yes / No**)   Does this surprise you? (**Yes / No**)   Why or why
     not?

4.   Review all the information you have gathered above. Would you consider investing in this company?
     Why or why not? Support your conclusion with sound reasoning.

Please note: Internet websites are constantly being updated; therefore, if the information is not found where indicated,
please explore the website further to find the information.

Activity 108   **COMPREHENSIVE COMPANY RESEARCH USING THE EDGAR DATABASE**
Using www.sec.gov

Purpose: · Use the EDGAR (Electronic Data Gathering, Analysis and Retrieval) database to
research information about a company.

This website provides access to reports required by the SEC (Securities and Exchange Commission) for
publicly traded companies. Required information includes a description of the business, products, and
services and financial statements with management's discussion and analysis.

1.   Under "About the SEC" click on *What We Do*.
      a.   *Identify* the primary mission of the U.S. Securities and Exchange Commission (SEC).

      b.   Review the other information presented and *comment* on one item that you find interesting.

2.   In the left-hand menu click on *Filings (EDGAR)* and then *Search for Company Filings* followed by
      Companies & Other Filings. Under "Enter your search information:" for *Company name:* type in
      Panera Bread Co and then click on *Find Companies*. Select the most recent **Form 10-K** (annual
      report) information by choosing the html format.

            Scroll down the page and record the following information:
            Company conformed name: _____
            Standard Industrial Classification (SIC Code Name):   _____
            Standard Industrial Classification number (SIC Code #): # _____
            State of Incorporation: _____
            Business Address – City and State: _____

3.   Scroll down and click on Document 1.

      a.   The Panera Bread Company was originally formed in March _____ under the name of
            _____.

      b.   At the end of the most recent year, Panera had _____ (number of) system-wide
            bakery-cafes of which most were (**company-owned / franchise-operated**).

            CONCEPT AND STRATEGY
      c.   The company's concept focuses on what?

      d.   What items are key to the success of the company?

MARKETING

e.   The company believes it competes on (**price / an entire experience**).

f.   The company measures its average check per transaction. At the company-owned bakery-cafes opened eighteen months or longer, the greatest average check per transaction was for (**breakfast / lunch / lunch in the evening**), which averaged $_____ per check.

g.   SITE SELECTION   What items are taken into consideration when selecting a site and why?

h.   MANAGEMENT INFORMATION SYSTEMS   What type of information is gathered for analysis by the computerized cash registers of the company-operated bakery-cafes?

i.   FRANCHISE OPERATIONS   To become a franchise owner the typical agreement requires how much up-front cash and continuing royalties?

4.   Review the CONSOLIDATED FINANCIAL STATEMENTS and record the following information for the two most recent years: _____ _____

a.   Total assets $_____ $_____

b.   Total revenues $_____ $_____

c.   Net income $_____ $_____

d.   Net cash provided by operating activities $_____ $_____

e.   The change in revenue is due to what? *Hint*: Refer to "Item 7. Management's Discussion and Analysis of Financial Condition and Results of Operations."

f.   What do the financial statement amounts recorded above indicate?

5.   Scroll through the information on the Form 10-K and *comment* on one item that you find interesting.

Please note: Internet websites are constantly being updated; therefore, if the information is not found where indicated, please explore the website further to find the information.

COMPREHENSIVE FINANCIAL STATEMENT RESEARCH
                      USING THE EDGAR DATABASE
                            Using www.sec.gov

Purpose: · Use the EDGAR (Electronic Data Gathering, Analysis and Retrieval) database
                 to research financial information about a company.

This website provides access to reports required by the SEC (Securities and Exchange Commission) for
publicly traded companies, including financial statements with management's discussion and analysis.

a.   Under *Filings and Forms (EDGAR)* click on *Search for Company Filings* followed by *Companies
       & Other Filings*. Under "Enter your search information:" for *Company name:* type in Panera
       Bread Co and then click on *Find Companies*. Select the most recent **Form 10-K** (annual report)
       information by choosing the html format.

b.   Scroll down and click on Document 1. Find the consolidated financial statements.
       Analyze the financial statements by answering the following questions:

Please note: Internet websites are constantly being updated; therefore, if the information is not found where indicated,
please explore the website further to find the information.

BALANCE SHEET

1.   At the most recent year end, how much is reported for:
           Total assets? $_____ thousand

           Total liabilities? $_____ thousand

           Total stockholders' equity? $_____ thousand

       Does the accounting equation hold true?   (**Yes / No**)   If not, why not?

2.   Which account contains the *largest* amount for:
           Assets?   _____

           Liabilities?   _____

           Stockholders' equity?   _____

       Briefly explain the most likely reason for each being the largest account.

3. At the most recent year end, how much have shareholders contributed in total for issued shares of:
    Common stock? $_____ thousand (excluding treasury stock)
    Preferred stock? $_____ thousand

    Total contributed capital was $_____ thousand for the earliest year reported and
    $_____ thousand for the most recent year reported. Since the earliest year reported, this
    account has (**increased / decreased**) by $_____ thousand, which is a _____%
    (**increase / decrease**).

    What might explain this change?

4. Retained earnings was $_____ thousand for the earliest year reported and
    $_____ thousand for the most recent year reported. Since the earliest year reported, this
    account has (**increased / decreased**) by $_____ thousand, which is a _____%
    (**increase / decrease**).

    What might explain this change?

5. Compute the **current ratio** for the last two years (Current assets / Current liabilities).
        (Most recent year) _____ _____
    This trend is generally considered (**favorable / unfavorable**).

    Does this company have the ability to pay its current debt? (**Yes / No**)

    What do these current ratios indicate?

6. Compute the **debt ratio** for the last two years (Total liabilities / Total assets).
        (Most recent year) _____ _____
    In general, the direction of this trend indicates that a company is assuming (**more / less**) financial risk.
    This company is primarily financing assets with (**debt / equity**).

    What might explain this choice of financing?

    What do these debt ratios indicate?

7. This balance sheet indicates a (**strong / weak**) financial position.
    Support your response with at least two observations.

INCOME STATEMENT

8. Total revenue was $_____ thousand for the earliest year reported and $_____ thousand for the most recent year reported. Since the earliest year reported, this account has (**increased / decreased**) by $_____ thousand, which is a _____% (**increase / decrease**).

    This company (**appears / does not appear**) to be competitive within its industry. How can you tell?

9. Net income was $_____ thousand for the earliest year reported and $_____ thousand for the most recent year reported. Since the earliest year reported, this account has (**increased / decreased**) by $_____ thousand, which is a _____% (**increase / decrease**).

10. Identify the three greatest expenses. Does this make sense? (**Yes / No**) Why?

11. Compute the **asset-turnover ratio** for the past two years (Total revenues / Total assets).
     (Most recent year) _____ _____

     This trend is (**favorable / unfavorable**). Why? What do these ratios indicate?

12. Compute the **return-on-sales ratio** (ROS) for the past two years (Net income / Total revenues).
     (Most recent year) _____ _____

     Revenues grew at a (**greater / lesser**) rate than expenses. How can you tell?

13. Compute the **return-on-assets ratio** (ROA) for the past two years (Net income / Total assets).
     (Most recent year) _____ _____

     This trend is (**favorable / unfavorable**). Why? What do these ratios indicate?

14. Compute the **return-on-equity ratio** (ROE) for the past two years (Net income / Total stockholders' equity).
     (Most recent year) _____ _____

     This trend is (**favorable / unfavorable**). Why? What do these ratios indicate?

15. Identify **basic earnings per common share** (EPS) for the past two years: $_____ $_____
     This trend is (**favorable / unfavorable**). Why? What do these ratios indicate?

16. This income statement indicates (**strong / weak**) profitability. Why?
     Support your response with at least two observations.

STATEMENT OF CASH FLOWS

17. At the most recent year end,

      $_____ thousand was (**provided / used**) by operating activities.

      $_____ thousand was (**provided / used**) by investing activities.

      $_____ thousand was (**provided / used**) by financing activities.

18. The primary source of cash was (**operating / investing / financing**) activities.
This is generally considered (**favorable / unfavorable**). Why?

19. For the most recent year, what is the primary *investing* activity?

The company is (**purchasing / selling**) more property and equipment. How can you tell?

20. For the most recent year, what is the primary *financing* activity?

The company is (**issuing / purchasing**) more common stock. How can you tell?

21. This statement of cash flows indicates a (**strong / weak**) cash position. Why?

NOTES to the financial statements

22. Refer to the Property and Equipment note. (Note 4 in the 2002 annual report.)

Regarding property and equipment for the most recent year, $_____ thousand was
reported as the acquisition cost, $_____ thousand was reported for accumulated
depreciation, and $_____ thousand was reported as the book value.

(**Acquisition cost / Book value**) is reported on the balance sheet and used in the calculation of total
assets.

23. Refer to the Accrued Expenses note. (Note 7 in the 2002 annual report.)

What is the greatest item within accrued expenses?

COMPREHENSIVE

24. Would you consider investing in this corporation? Why or why not?
Your conclusion should be comprehensive and supported by sound reasoning.

CHAPTER 10

CORPORATE ANALYSIS

PURPOSE: Chapter 10 is a capstone project that includes researching and analyzing a publicly traded corporation of the student's choice. This project is divided into four parts. In Part I, students research and describe their company's primary business activities in addition to providing information regarding the company's history, position within their industry, competition, recent developments, and future direction. In Part II a ten-year market analysis is completed. Part III requires research into industry norms for commonly used ratios. In Part IV the corporate financial statements are analyzed using trend analysis and common-size statement techniques. Parts V and VI ask the student to answer the question, "Would you advise a friend to invest in this company?" Each part requires at least a one-page written analysis. These analyses must be individually written with each student submitting a separate report.

Have fun with this project! Be creative! Include graphs, charts, and other items to enhance the overall project.

If you are undecided regarding which company to select, below is a listing of the 30 corporations comprising the Dow Jones Industrial Average (DJIA) plus other corporations that you may find of interest.

"30 INDUSTRIAL" STOCKS
that currently comprise the
DOW JONES INDUSTRIAL AVERAGE

AT&T	COCA COLA	HEWLETT-PACKARD	MCDONALDS
ALCOA	COMPANY	HOME DEPOT	MERCK
ALTRIA GROUP	DISNEY (WALT)	HONEYWELL	MICROSOFT
AMERICAN	DUPONT	IBM	PROCTER & GAMBLE
EXPRESS	EASTMAN KODAK	INTEL	SBC COMMUNICATIONS
BOEING	EXXON MOBIL CORP	INTERNATIONAL PAPER	3M
CATERPILLAR	GENERAL ELECTRIC	JOHNSON & JOHNSON	UNITED TECHNOLOGIES
CITIGROUP	GENERAL MOTORS	JP MORGAN CHASE	WAL-MART

OTHER CORPORATIONS

Advanced Micro Devices	Dow Chemical	Lilly (Eli)	Pfizer
Amazon.com	FedEx Corp	Liz Claiborne	Pitney Bowes
American Greetings	Ford Motor Co	Lockheed Martin	Qualcomm
American Home Products	Fossil, Inc.	LSI Logic	Royal Caribbean Cruises
Amgen	Gannett	Lucent Technologies	Reebok International
AMR (American Airlines)	Gap, Inc. (The)	Mattel	Sara Lee
Anheuser-Busch	General Mills	May Dept Stores	Sears, Roebuck & Co
AOL Time Warner	Gillette	MCI	Smucker Co. (The J.M.)
Barnes & Noble, Inc.	Harley-Davidson	Monsanto	Southwest Airlines
Best Buy	Hasbro	Motorola	Starbucks
Borders Group	Hershey Foods	Nike Inc.	Sun Microsystems
Brinker International	Heinz (HJ)	Nucor	Toys R Us
Bristol-Meyers Squibb	IHOP	Office Depot	Walgreen Co
Callaway Golf	Kimberly-Clark	Oracle	Waste Management
Circuit City Stores	Kmart	Outback Steakhouse	Wrigley (Wm.) Jr.
Costco Wholesale	Kellogg	Panera Bread	Xerox Corp
Deckers Outdoor	Kroger	Papa John's	Yahoo! Inc
Dell Computer	Lauder (Estee)	PepsiCo	Yum! Brand

Activity 110   **PART I: TELL ME ABOUT YOUR COMPANY**

Purpose: · Use a variety of resources to research a corporation.
                      · Prepare a well-written paper describing your corporation.

Requirements:

A.   **Research and then describe your company's primary business activities.** Also include a brief
       historical summary, a list of competitors, the company's position within the industry, recent
       developments within the company/industry, future direction, and other items of significance to your
       corporation.

B.   **Include information from a variety of resources.**

       1.   **Consult the Form 10-K filed with the SEC.** This form contains a wealth of information.
              Read through *Item 1. Business Summary* to locate information regarding the business,
              product offerings, marketing strategy, competition, and market share. Available at
              www.sec.gov.

       2.   **Review the Annual Report** and be certain to read through the *Letter to Shareholders,*
              which summarizes the past year and highlights future opportunities. Annual Reports are
              generally available online at the company's website in the investor relations section.

       3.   **Explore the corporate website.** A corporate website usually provides updated,
              comprehensive information including links to current news items and financial information.
              Note that the company provides the information posted on the website and, therefore, may
              be biased in favor of the company.

       4.   **Select *at least two* significant news items from recent business periodicals.** Examples of
              business periodicals include *The Wall Street Journal, Forbes, Fortune, Inc.,* and *Business
              Week.* Many of these periodicals are available at the library in hard copy and also online.

       5.   **Use information from *at least one* financial service**:
              Library references: a.   *The Value Line Investment Survey*
                                      b.   *Standard and Poor's Stock Reports or Industry Surveys*
                                      c.   *Mergent's Industry Review*
              Internet resources: d.   www.hoovers.com
                                      e.   moneycentral.msn.com
                                      f.   and other financial websites

              These services provide a historical summary, description of the primary business activities,
              recent developments, and select financial information about publicly-traded companies.

C.   **Submit a report that is two to five pages long.** The report should be well written with introductory
       and concluding paragraphs. References must be appropriately cited.
       Format: Double-spaced, one-inch margins, using a 12-point Times-New-Roman font.

D.   **In the appendix**, appropriately identify and place photocopies or a computer printout of the
       material used for your report noting the source. Highlight significant information. Incorporate this
       information into your report.

E.   **Recommended prerequisites**: Activities 100, 101, 108

PART II: MARKET RESEARCH

Purpose: · Research the current stock quote of your company and analyze past market activity.
· Summarize market activity results.

Requirements:

A.   **Research the stock market** activity of your company's stock, including the current stock quote and past market activity over (at least) the most recent 10 years.

B.   **Summarize the results in a one-page report.**
Format: Double-spaced, one-inch margins, using a 12-point Times-New-Roman font.

C.   **In the appendix**, appropriately identify and place photocopies or a computer printout of the material used for your report noting the source. Highlight significant information.

D.   **Recommended prerequisites**: Activities 106,107

Activity 112 **PART III: COMPUTE RATIOS AND COMPARE TO INDUSTRY NORMS**

Purpose: · Research the primary SIC (Standard Industrial Classification) Code for your company.
· Use resources available to obtain industry averages for commonly used ratios.
· Compare company ratio results to industry averages.
· Prepare a well-written report summarizing the ratio analysis using appropriate business and accounting vocabulary.

Requirements:

A. **Obtain the four-digit primary SIC (Standard Industrial Classification) Code for your company.** Enter the primary SIC code at the top of the last column on the Ratio Analysis Worksheet. The Standard Industrial Classification code is a coding system used to report information on U.S. businesses. It divides corporations into 10 major groups that are further divided into major categories. Many corporations engage in more than one type of business. The primary SIC code refers to the type of business with the largest volume of sales. The secondary SIC codes are listed in descending order according to sales volume. *Hint*: Refer to Activity 100 that uses www.hoovers.com to identify the SIC code.

B. **Obtain industry averages for commonly used ratios**. Industry average information is generally reported by SIC code. Record the industry averages available for your company in the last column of the Ratios Analysis Worksheet. Resources for industry average information include:

Library references:
Almanac of Business and Industrial Financial Ratios, by Leo Troy, published by Prentice Hall
Industry Norms and Key Business Ratios, Dun and Bradstreet, Inc.
Standard and Poor's Industry Surveys
Mergent's Industry Review
Internet resources:
moneycentral.msn.com (Refer to Activity 105)
Other financial websites

C. **Obtain and/or calculate all of the ratios listed on the Ratio Analysis Worksheet for the three most recent years of information.** Use the attached forms or facsimiles.

D. **Submit a report that is at least one page long.** The report should be a well-written paper that (1) comments on significant amounts, trends, and relationships of the three years of ratio information, and (2) compares the company ratios to industry averages.
Format: Double-spaced, one-inch margins, using a 12-point Times-New-Roman font.

E. **In the appendix**, appropriately identify and place photocopies or a computer printout of the industry average information used for your report noting the source. Include any manual computations of the corporate ratios. Highlight significant information.

F. **Recommended prerequisites**: Activities 100, 105

Activity 113 **PART IV: PREPARE FINANCIAL STATEMENTS IN CONDENSED FORMAT AND A WRITTEN ANALYSIS**

Purpose:
· Use resources available to obtain financial statements for the past four fiscal years.
· Prepare a classified balance sheet, multi-step income statement, and the statement of cash flows using the condensed format provided.
· Prepare trend analyses and common-size statements.
· Prepare a well-written analysis of each financial statement using appropriate business and accounting vocabulary.

Requirements:

A.   **Obtain the financial statements for the past four fiscal years for the company you selected.** Financial statements are available from a variety of online sources including:
        yahoo.multexinvestor.com (Refer to Activity 102)
        edgarscan.pwcglobal.com/servlets/edgarscan (Refer to Activity 103)
        www.sec.gov (Refer to Activity 109)

B.   **Prepare a multi-step income statement, classified balance sheet, and statement of cash flows in condensed format.** Condensed means some accounts are grouped into one summarized subtotal, but no numbers are left out of the computations. Each financial statement should total properly. Use the attached forms or facsimiles.

C.   **Prepare common-size statements and trend analyses for both the income statement and the balance sheet.** Use the attached forms or facsimiles.

D.   **Submit at least one page of written analysis for *each* financial statement.** The report should be well written using appropriate business and accounting vocabulary. Comment on significant amounts, trends, and relationships. When appropriate, reference amounts from the common-size statements and trend analyses. *Format*: Double-spaced, one-inch margins, using a 12-point Times-New-Roman font.

E.   **In the appendix,** appropriately identify and place photocopies or a computer printout of the financial statement information used noting the source. Highlight significant information.

F.   **Recommended prerequisites:** Activities 102, 103, 104, 109

Activity 114   **PART V:**   *WRITTEN REPORT*: **WOULD YOU ADVISE A FRIEND TO INVEST IN THIS COMPANY?**

Purpose: · Base a recommendation on previous research, analysis, and sound reasoning.
                  · Prepare a well-written report using appropriate business and accounting vocabulary.

Requirements:

A.   Prepare a written report based upon your research and analysis of this company's financial information, **"Would you advise a friend to invest in this company?"** Support your answer with a comprehensive explanation incorporating sound reasoning. Your advice should be well written with introductory and concluding paragraphs. References should be appropriately cited.

B.   **Submit a report that is at least two pages long.** The report should be well written with introductory and concluding paragraphs. References must be appropriately cited. *Format*: Double-spaced, one-inch margins, using a 12-point Times-New-Roman font.

Activity 115   **PART VI:**   *PRESENTATION*: **WOULD YOU ADVISE A FRIEND TO INVEST IN THIS COMPANY?**

Purpose: · Base a recommendation on previous research, analysis, and sound reasoning.
                  · Prepare a presentation using one visual aid.

Requirements:

A.   **Prepare a presentation** based upon your research and analysis of this company's financial information, **"Would you advise a friend to invest in this company?"**
  •   The presentation should present historical, competitive, and financial research that supports advice about investing in your company.
  •   Share only the significant *highlights* of your research. (Notice I did not say a summary.)
  •   The presentation should be delivered well with introductory and concluding paragraphs.
  •   Students, who are not attentive and courteous during the presentations, may be downgraded on their presentations.

B.   **Present a five to eight minute oral presentation to the class that keeps the attention of the audience.** Five points are awarded for staying within the 5-8 minute time limit, zero points if not.

C.   **Use at least one visual aid** (PowerPoint slides, props, etc.)

D.   **In the appendix** provide a copy of PowerPoint slides and other written visual aids for the instructor.

E.   **Recommended prerequisites**: Activities 86 – 91 using Excel and PowerPoint

APPENDIX

Be creative! Include graphs, charts, pictures, and other items to enhance the overall project. Additional points may be awarded (up to the maximum) for additional information provided and creativity. Remember to also include copies of the documentation requested in Parts I through VI.

Company Name: _____

CONDENSED
CLASSIFIED BALANCE SHEET

Dated: ($ in millions)	(Most recent year)	‑‑‑‑‑‑‑	‑‑‑‑‑‑‑	‑‑‑‑‑‑‑
Current assets	$	$	$	$
Property, plant, and equipment, net				
Other assets				
TOTAL assets	$	$	$	$

Current liabilities	$	$	$	$
Long-term liabilities				
Contributed capital				
Retained earnings				
Treasury stock and other stockholders' equity				
TOTAL liabilities and stockholders' equity	$	$	$	$

Company Name: _____

CONDENSED CLASSIFIED BALANCE SHEET
Common-Size Statements

Dated: ($ in millions)	(Most recent year)	----------	----------	----------
Current assets	%	%	%	%
Property, plant, and equipment, net	%	%	%	%
Other assets	%	%	%	%
TOTAL assets	100.0 %	100.0 %	100.0 %	100.0 %

Current liabilities	%	%	%	%
Long-term liabilities	%	%	%	%
Contributed capital	%	%	%	%
Retained earnings	%	%	%	%
Treasury stock and other stockholders' equity	%	%	%	%
TOTAL liabilities and stockholders' equity	100.0 %	100.0 %	100.0 %	100.0 %

Company Name: _____

CONDENSED CLASSIFIED BALANCE SHEET
Trend Analysis

Dated: ($ in millions)	══════ ══════ (Most recent year)	‒‒‒‒‒‒	‒‒‒‒‒‒	‒‒‒‒‒‒
Current assets				100
Property, plant, and equipment, net				100
Other assets				100
TOTAL assets				100

Current liabilities				100
Long-term liabilities				100
Contributed capital				100
Retained earnings				100
Treasury stock and other stockholders' equity				100
TOTAL liabilities and stockholders' equity				100

Company Name: _____

CONDENSED
MULTI-STEP INCOME STATEMENT

Fiscal year ended: ($ in millions)	‾‾‾‾‾‾‾‾ ‾‾‾‾‾‾‾‾ (Most recent year)	_____	_____	_____
Net sales	$	$	$	$
Cost of goods sold				
Gross margin				
Operating expenses				
Income from operations				
Other gains and losses				
Income before income tax				
Income tax expense				
Income before nonrecurring items				
Nonrecurring items				
Net income	$	$	$	$

Earnings per share				

Company Name: _____

CONDENSED MULTI-STEP INCOME STATEMENT
Common-Size Statements

Fiscal year ended: ($ in millions)	(Most recent year)			
Net sales	100.0 %	100.0 %	100.0 %	100.0 %
Cost of goods sold	%	%	%	%
Gross margin	%	%	%	%
Operating expenses	%	%	%	%
Income from operations	%	%	%	%
Other gains and losses	%	%	%	%
Income before income tax	%	%	%	%
Income tax expense	%	%	%	%
Income before nonrecurring items	%	%	%	%
Nonrecurring items	%	%	%	%
Net income	%	%	%	%

Company Name: _____

CONDENSED MULTI-STEP INCOME STATEMENT
Trend Analysis

Fiscal year ended: ($ in millions)	‾‾‾‾ ‾‾‾‾ (Most recent year)	– – – –	– – – –	– – – –
Net sales				100
Cost of goods sold				100
Gross margin				100
Operating expenses				100
Income from operations				100
Other gains and losses				100
Income before income tax				100
Income tax expense				100
Income before nonrecurring items				100
Nonrecurring items				100
Net income				100

Earnings per share				100

Company Name: _____

CONDENSED
STATEMENT OF CASH FLOWS

Fiscal year ended: ($ in millions)	_____ (most recent year)	_____	_____	_____
Net cash inflows (outflows) from **operating activities**	$	$	$	$
Net cash inflows (outflows) from **investing activities**				
Net cash inflows (outflows) from **financing activities**				
Effect of **exchange rate** on cash				
Net change in cash equivalents				
Cash equivalents at year start				
Cash equivalents at year end	$	$	$	$

Company Name: _____

RATIO ANALYSIS WORKSHEET

Fiscal year ended:	————— (Most recent year)	—————	—————	SIC #_____ **Industry Average**
1. Current ratio				
2. Acid-test ratio (Quick ratio)				
3. Inventory turnover				
4. Accounts receivable turnover				
5. Days' sales in receivables				
6. Debt ratio				
7. Times-interest-earned ratio				
8. Return on sales				
9. Return on assets				
10. Return on common stockholders' equity				
11. Earnings per share of common stock				
12. Price/earnings ratio				
13. Dividend yield				
14. Book value per share of common stock				

PART V: WRITTEN PROJECT GRADE SHEET

Name _____   Company _____

POINTS

_____/20   **PART I** (Act 110) Tell me about your company
Primary business activity
Historical summary
Competitors / Position within the industry
Recent developments and other significant information
2-5 pages, typed and double-spaced

_____/10   **PART II** (Act 111) Market research
Current stock quote
10-year analysis
One-page summary

_____/ 10   **PART III** (Act 112) Compute ratios and compare to industry norms
Ratio computations
Industry averages (at least nine, all ratios do not apply to all industries)
One-page written analysis

PART IV (Act 113) Prepare financial statements in condensed format and a written analysis

_____/10   *Income Statement*, Common-size statements, Trend analysis
One-page written analysis

_____/10   *Balance Sheet*, Common-size statements, Trend analysis
One-page written analysis

_____/10   *Statement Of Cash Flows*
One-page written analysis
Typed and double-spaced

_____/ 10   **PART V** (Act 114) Would you advise a friend to invest in this corporation?
Conclusion supported by sound reasoning
Comprehensive
At least 2 pages, typed and double-spaced

_____/ 10   **APPENDIX**   Significant information highlighted
Part I: 2 news items highlighted, 1 financial service resource highlighted
Other significant resources highlighted
Part II: Market research items highlighted
Part III: Industry average information and ratio computations
Part IV: Copies of the financial statements

_____/ 10   **OTHER**   Well-organized
Good writing style, good grammar, 12-point Times-New-Roman font
Attractive and creative
Effective use of graphs and charts

_____/100   **TOTAL SCORE**

PART VI: PRESENTATION GRADE SHEET

Points Possible	Points Awarded	ITEM	DESCRIPTION
Student name:			Company:
10		OPENING AND CLOSING	Opening should grab the audience's attention. Closing is evident and leaves a definite impression of your investment advice.
10		AUDIENCE APPEAL	Interesting to the audience Audience is attentive and can easily follow
25		CONTENT	Body -- State what you are going to say, say it, and then summarize what you just said Main points are supported with good explanation and examples Knowledgeable about the company/subject Information is accurate Highlights presented, not a summary of the project Well organized Direct link to accounting should be obvious
10		PRESENTATION	Appropriate eye contact with the audience Note cards may be used, but not read Professional appearance Gestures that are appropriate and not distracting Feet are planted squarely on the ground Sense of humor
10		VOICE	Voice is projected to the back row Speaks slowly and clearly Professional language Few "ums" and "okays" Energetic
10		VISUAL AID (*Please provide a copy for the instructor*)	Effectively supports content Attractive Creative Not more than 1 PowerPoint slide per minute (max 8) Not cluttered – not more than 7 items across and 7 items down
10		ADVICE	Investing advice is clearly stated and well-supported
0 or 5		TIME LIMIT	5-8 Minutes
10		QUESTION AND ANSWER	Knowledgeable enough to answer questions Sufficient response Student presentations: Ask at least one question per class regarding other student presentations.
100		**Total Points**	